Acclaim for Maxine Hong Kingston's

I Love a Broad Margin to My Life

"Delights as an unconventional, intimate and intensely personal life story. . . . Forcing a slower, calmer contemplation of Hong Kingston's words." —*The Miami Herald*

"Moving. . . . Whether she's recalling the birth of her son or the time she was arrested for protesting the Iraq war, Kingston's memories are pungent and vivid." —*The Post and Courier*

"She leads the reader on a tour of her native China, her rich language often matching the lushness of the landscape itself. . . . Effortlessly transitions from personal experience to the worlds of her characters. . . . As much an examination of the nature of time and aging as it is an exploration of cultural identity and origin, *I Love a Broad Margin to My Life* contains both moments of dark alienation and buoyant transcendence." —*Time Out New York*

"Blurring the lines among poetry, fiction, and memoir. . . . A meditation on form and formlessness, on meaning and identity, and how the most essential truths often exist outside the boundaries, in something of an ur-state." —*Los Angeles Times*

"She seems at peace with the necessary sacrifices and negotiations she's made as a writer, wife and mother. Yet she's also acutely aware of her mortality and determined to carve out the free time to which she feels entitled at last. . . . Written in a dreamlike, impressionistic style. . . . Takes on a kind of mythical quality."
—*The Boston Globe*

"Engaging. . . . Startling." —Heller McAlpin, NPR

"A sprawling, globe-hopping long poem. . . . Kingston is thinking deeply about the act of writing itself. . . . I found myself compelled by Kingston's efforts to capture the disjointed landscape wrought by globalization. . . . Touching. . . . Offers its readers a memorable set of images, narratives, and questions that continue to push against the foundations of memoir, just as her earlier work, *The Woman Warrior,* did four decades earlier."
—*Hyphen Magazine*

"A brilliantly penned memoir. . . . She shares cultural experiences with a primal pentameter that may equal or surpass anything her readers have ever experienced." —*San Francisco Book Review*

Maxine Hong Kingston

I Love a Broad Margin to My Life

Maxine Hong Kingston is the author of *The Woman Warrior,* *China Men, Tripmaster Monkey,* and *The Fifth Book of Peace,* among other works. She is the recipient of numerous awards, including the National Book Award, the National Book Critics Circle award, the presidentially conferred National Humanities Medal, the Medal for Distinguished Contribution to American Letters from the National Book Foundation, and the F. Scott Fitzgerald Award. For many years a Senior Lecturer for Creative Writing at UC Berkeley, she lives in Oakland, California.

INTERNATIONAL

I Love a Broad Margin to My Life

Maxine Hong Kingston

VINTAGE INTERNATIONAL · VINTAGE BOOKS
A DIVISION OF RANDOM HOUSE, INC. · NEW YORK

FIRST VINTAGE INTERNATIONAL EDITION, FEBRUARY 2011

Copyright © 2011 by Maxine Hong Kingston

Calligraphy by the author.

Grateful acknowledgment is made to the following for permission to reprint previously published material:

Coleman Barks: Excerpt from "Song of the Reed" from The Essential Rumi, translated by Coleman Barks. Reprinted by permission of Coleman Barks.

Irving Berlin Music Company: Excerpt from "Sittin' in the Sun (Countin' My Money)" by Irving Berlin, copyright © 1953 by Irving Berlin. Copyright renewed. International copyright secured. All rights reserved. Reprinted by permission of Irving Berlin Music Company.

The Library of Congress has cataloged the Alfred A. Knopf edition as follows:
Kingston, Maxine Hong.
I love a broad margin to my life / by Maxine Hong Kingston.—1st ed.
p.   cm.
  1. Kingston, Maxine Hong.   2. Authors, American—20th century—
Biography.   3. Chinese American authors—Biography.   4. Chinese
American Women—Biography.   I. Title.
PS3561.I52Z46 2011
818'.54—dc22

Vintage ISBN: 978-0-307-45459-1

www.vintagebooks.com

Printed in the United States of America
10   9   8   7   6   5   4   3   2   1

To the Ancestors and

my contemporaries and

our children

I Love a Broad Margin to My Life

HOME

I am turning 65 years of age.
In 2 weeks I will be 65 years old.
I can accumulate time *and* lose
time? I sit here writing in the dark—
can't see to change these penciled words—
just like my mother, alone, bent over her writing,
just like my father bent over his writing, alone
but for me watching. She got out of bed,
wrapped herself in a blanket, and wrote down
the strange sounds Father, who was dead,
was intoning to her. He was reading aloud

calligraphy that he'd written—carved with inkbrush—
on his tombstone. She wasn't writing in answer.
She wasn't writing a letter. Who was she writing to?
Nobody.

                This well-deep outpouring is not *for*
anything. Yet we have to put into exact words
what we are given to see, hear, know.
Mother's eyesight blurred; she saw trash
as flowers. "Oh. How very beautiful."
She was lucky, seeing beauty, living
in beauty, whether or not it was there.

I am often looking in mirrors, and singling
out my face in group photographs.
Am I pretty at 65?
What does old look like?
Sometimes I am wrinkled, sometimes not.
So much depends upon lighting.
A camera crew shot pictures of me—one of
"5 most influential people over 60
in the East Bay." I am homely; I am old.
I look like a tortoise in a curly white wig.
I am stretching head and neck toward
the light, such effort to lift the head, to open

the eyes. Black, shiny, lashless eyes.
Talking mouth. I must utter you
something. My wrists are crossed in my lap;
wrinkles run up the left forearm.
(It's my right shoulder that hurts—Rollerblading
accident—does the pain show, does my hiding it?)
I should've spoken up, Don't take
my picture, not in that glare. One side
of my neck and one cheek are gone in black
shadow. Nobody looks good in hard focus,
high contrast—black sweater and skirt,
white hair, white sofa, white
curtains. My colors and my home, but rearranged.
The crew had pushed the reds and blues and greens aside.
The photographer, a young woman, said, "Great. Great."
From within my body, I can't sense that crease
on my left cheek. I have to get—win—
compliments. "You are beautiful." "So cute."
"Such a kind face." "You are simple."
"You move fast." "Chocolate Chip."
A student I taught long ago
called me Chocolate Chip. And only yesterday
a lifelong friend told Earll, my husband,
he's lucky, he's got me—the Chocolate Chip.

They mean, I think, my round face
and brown-bead eyes. I keep
count. I mind that I be good-looking.
I don't want to look like Grandmother,
Ah Po. Her likeness is the mask of tragedy.
"An ape weeps when another ape weeps."
She is Ancestress; she is prayed to. She
sits, the queen, center of the family in China,
center of the family portrait (my mother in it too,
generations of in-laws around her)—all
is black and white but for a dot of jade-green
at Po's ears, and a curve of jade-green
at her wrist. Lotus lily feet show
from the hem of her gown. She wanted to be
a beauty. She lived to be 100.
My mother lived to be 100. "One
hundred and three," she said. Chinese
lie about their age, making themselves older.
Or maybe she was 97 when the lady official
from Social Security visited her, as the government visits
everyone who claims a 100th birthday.
MaMa showed off; she pedaled her exercise
bike, hammer-curled hot pink barbells.
Suddenly stopped—what if So-so Security

won't believe she's a century old?
Here's a way for calculating age: Subtract
from her age of death my age now.

$$100 - 65 = 35$$

I am 35 years-to-go.
                    Lately, I've been
writing a book a decade; I have time
to write 3 more books. Jane Austen
wrote 6 books. I've written 6 books.
Hers are 6 big ones, mine
4 big ones and 2 small ones.
I take refuge in numbers. I
waste my time with sudoku.
Day dawns, I am greedy, helpless
to begin 6-star difficulty
sudoku. Sun goes
down; I'm still stuck for that square
that will let the numbers fly into place.
What good am I getting out
of this? I'm not stopping time. Nothing
to show for my expenditures. Pure nothing.

8 days before my birthday, I went
to John Mulligan's funeral. He was 10

years younger than me. He died without
finishing his book, *MIAmerica*.
(I have a superstition that as long as I,
any writer, have things to write, I keep living.)
I joined in singing again and again
a refrain, "Send thou his soul to God." Earll,
though, did not sing, did not
say any of the Latin, any of the prayers.
He muttered that the Catholic Church divides you
against yourself, against your sexy body.
"The Church is a gyp." John Mulligan should've
been given a pagan ceremony; Woman Warrior,
Robert Louis Stevenson, and Cuchulain

had come to him in Viet Nam. John
carried them, tied to him by silver cords,
to the U.S. The priest, who came from the Philippines,
kept reminding one and all that the benefits
he was offering were for "Christians" only. But
he did observe John's being born and raised
in Scotland, and coming to America at 17.
Summarily drafted to Viet Nam. You
didn't have to be a citizen to be drafted.
He lived homeless for a while. He wrote his
way home. Died only a week ago,
run over walking across a highway.

.   .   .

The war count, as of today:

> Almost 2,000 killed in Iraq. G.I.s.
> Not counting Afghanis,
>> Iraqis,
>>
>> civilians,
>>
>> mercenaries,
>>
>> children, babies,
>>
>> journalists.

7 days before my birthday, I had breakfast with
Mary Gordon, who's always saying things
I never thought before: "It's capitalistic
of us to expect any good from peace demonstrations,
as if ritual has to have use, gain, profit."
I agreed, "Yes, it's Buddhist to go parading
for the sake of parading." "Can you think of a writer
(besides Chekhov) who is holy *and* an artist?"
"Grace Paley." She smiled. "Well, yes."
Obviously. "Thoreau." "Oh, no. Thoreau's
too Protestant, tidy, nonsexual. He goes
home to Mom for hot chocolate. No

sex, no tragedy, no humor."
Come to think of it, Thoreau doesn't make
me laugh. A line from *Walden* hangs over one
of my desks:

I love a broad margin to my life.

Sitting here at this sidewalk café with Mary,
deliberately taking time off from writing
and teaching duties, I am making a broad margin
to my life. The margin will be broader when we part,
and I am alone. Thoreau swam, then sat in the doorway
of his "Shelter," "large box," "dwelling-house,"
alone all the summer morning, rapt
in the sunlight and the trees and the stillness.
Birds flitted through the house. ". . . Until
by the sun falling in at my west window,
or the noise of some traveller's wagon on the distant
highway, I was reminded of the lapse of time."
I have a casita of my own, built instead of
a garage after the Big Fire. Its width
is the same as Thoreau's (10 feet), its length
a yard longer. He had a loft; I have
a skylight. I want to be a painter.

Sometimes, I hear the freeway, now and again
the train, and the campanile. Thoreau heard
the band playing military music; his neighbors
were going to war against Mexico. He made up his mind
not to pay taxes.
                    Trying broad-
margin meditation, I sit in
the sunny doorway of my casita, amidst the yucca
and loquats and purple rain birches. Some trees I
planted, some volunteered. Birds—
chickadees, finches, sparrows, pairs of doves,
a pair of towhees, and their enemy, the jay. Hawk
overhead. Barn swallows at twilight.
I know: Thoreau sat with notebook
and pencil in hand. Days full of writing.

> Days full of wanting.
> Let them go by without worrying
> that they do. Stay where you are
> inside such a pure hollow note.
>
> —RUMI

Evening, at an Oxfam Relief benefit
for Hurricane Katrina refugees, I read aloud

what Gilgamesh of Uruk (Iraq!) heard about a flood.
The Euphrates flattened a city ". . . bringing calamity
down on those whom now the sea engulfs
and overwhelms, my children who are now the children
of fishes." Earll auctioned away a 100th
anniversary Mardi Gras doubloon handed down
from his family. A bakery donated an immense cake
with candles, and people sang Happy Birthday to me.

6 days ahead of birthday: A small
white man sat abandoned at the stairs
to our garden. Summer sportcoat. It's autumn.
He carried a heavy suitcase.
Two bigger suitcases, trunk-size,
sat on the sidewalk. "Here B
and B?" he asked, and handed me papers.
Lists of bed-and-breakfasts, the top one
with our cross-street but no address number.
A neighbor must be running a secret B & B.
"Widow B and B." A widow used to
live next door, but her house burned
down, and we bought her vacant lot.
And there's a Viet Nam widow down the street,
and a faculty-wife widow 2 doors up.

"I got reservation. My name is Fred.
I came to see about my Social Security."
Where are you from? You can go to your local
Social Security office. "I came from
airport. I paid shuttle thirty-one
dollars." But it doesn't cost nearly that
to be driven here from OAK or
SFO. "Shuttle van brought
me here, to B and B." Earll looked
in the Yellow Pages, phoned some home-inns,
and drove Fred to a B & B, which cost $125
a night. "One hundred and
twenty-five dollars a *week*," Fred
corrected. No, no, a *day*. He
looked ready to cry. "Get me
a taxi." The innkeeper called motels, and found
Days Inn at $90 per night,
and a hotel at $60 per night.
Fred told us of his life: He had been educated
at San José State. He lived in a basement,
and studied engineering. He'd made $900
a month, then in San Francisco $1,200
a month. Housing was $30 a night.
"There's no work for engineers in San Francisco

anymore." Social Security will give
him $600 every month.
Earll also—$600 per month.
"In Iran, I live for a long time
on six hundred dollars." We took
Fred to BART. Go to San Francisco.
At a big hotel, ask for a "youth hostel."
Earll gave him a hug goodbye.
We picture the little lost man, from Iran,
getting his bags stuck in the turnstile,
leaving 1 or 2 behind as the train
doors shut. Should've warned him, he has to
compete with the Katrina refugees' $2,000
housing allowance. Should've offered him water.
In Fred's reality: Widows rent out rooms.
At B & B on the computer, hit
Print—voilà—room reserved,
room confirmed. Taxi drivers know
the place for you, and will take you to it.
Everywhere wander people who have not
the ability to handle this world.

Late the next day, we went to the City
for me to talk on the radio about veterans of war,

veterans of peace. In a waiting room, women
in scarves—Muslims—were serving food to one
another. Each one seemed to have come from
a different land and race, her headdress
and style and skin color unlike any sister's.
Silks. Velvet. Poly jacquard. Coral,
red and black, henna, aqua. Peacock.
Crystals, rhinestones. Gold thread. Impossibly
diverse cultures, yet Islam brings them together.
This corridor is an oasis on the Silk Road,
as if that thoroughfare continues through Africa,
and across oceans. An Egyptian-looking woman
held up to me, then to Earll,
a tray of fruits and vegetables. "Eid,"
she said. "Celebrate the Eid."
I chose a cherry tomato and a medjool date.
I willed my Thank you to embrace her, go through
and around her, and enfold the other Muslims, the ones
here, and the many far away. Thank you,
Muslims, for giving food to whoever happens
among you. I'm lucky, my timing in sync with their time,
the sun setting, and a new moon coming up.
Last day of Ramadan, women ending their fast.
If not for years of practicing Buddhist silence

and Quaker silence, I would've chattered away,
and missed the quiet, the peace, the lovingkindness.
Happy birthday to me.
                              Sunday, my friend Claude
brought a tea grown by old Greek ladies.
"It cures everything." I drink, though nothing
needs curing. "Cured!" we said in unison.
Monday ere birthday, I resolve: I shall rest
from worry and pursuit. (In childhood chasedreams,
monsters chased me. Now, I do the chasing.)
Joseph, our son, calls. In a marathon read,
he's finished all the books I've ever published.

I'm the only writer I know whose offspring
reads her. "How was it?" "Good." ("Accurate,"
said my mother.) Joseph cares for accuracy too.
He's mailing me pages of errata: I got
the Hawaiian wrong; I got the pidgin
wrong. He's a musician; he has the ear. I love
hearing his voice wishing me Happy Birthday.
"I must be getting old too; I
really like my power tools." He'd
read again and again the instructions on how
to use a chainsaw, then cut up the pine
trees without mishap. Borders in Honolulu

sold all his CDs, and wants more.

My time in Hawai'i, I never learned the hula,

never learned the language. Couldn't bear

the music. Heard at evening, the music—mele

and pila ho'okani—would stay with me

all the night and into the next day.

It hurt my chest; my chest filled with tears.

Words for the feeling are: Regret. Minamina.

(*Hun,* said my mother. *Hun,* the sound of want.

Hun.) *Hun* the nation, lost. *Hun*

the land. *Hun* the beloved, loving people.

They're dancing, feasting, talking-story, singing,

singing hello / goodbye. No sooner

hello than goodbye. Trees, fronds wave;

ocean waves. The time-blowing wind

smells of flowers and volcano. My son has given

me the reading that I never gave my father. Why

aren't writers read by their own children?

The child doesn't want to know that the parent

suffers, the parent is far, far away.

Joseph says, "Don't write about me."

"Okay. I won't do it anymore."

To read my father, I'd have to learn Chinese,

the most difficult of languages, each word a study.

A stroke off, a dot off, and you lose the word.

You get sent down for re-education. You lose your life.

My father wrote to me, poet to poet.

He replied to me. I had goaded

him: I'll tell about you, you silent man.

I'll suppose you. You speak up if I've got

you wrong. He answered me; he wrote

in the flyleaves and wide margins of the Chinese

editions of my books. I should've asked him to read

his poetry to me, and to say them in common speech.

I had had the time but not the nerve.

(Oh, but the true poet crosses eternal

distances. Perfect reader, come though 1,000

years from now. Poem can also reach

reader born 1,000 years *before*

the poem, wished into being. Li Bai

and Du Fu, lucky sea turtles,

found each other within their lifetimes.

Oh, the hopes of Chinese time

and Chinese poets. You don't have

to be a poet; you live in the turning

and returning cosmos this way: An act

of love I do this morning saves a life

on a far future battlefield. And the surprising

love I feel that saves my life comes from
a person whose soul somehow corresponding
with my soul doing me a good deed 1,000
years ago.) Cold, gray October
day. I've built a fire, and sit by it.
The last fire. Wood fires are being
banned. Drinking the tea that cures everything.
It's raining, drizzly enough, I need
not water the garden or go out to weed.
Do nothing all the perfect day.
A list of tasks for the rest of my working life:
Translate Father's writing into English.
Publish fine press editions of the books

with his calligraphy in the margins and
my translations and my commentary
on his commentary, like the I Ching. Father had
a happy life; happy people are always
making something. Learn how to grow
old and leave life. How to leave
you who love me? Do so in story.
For the writer, doing something in fiction
is the same as doing it in life.

. . .

I can make the hero of my quondam novel,
Monkey King, Wittman Ah Sing,
observe Hindu tradition, and on his 5–times–12
birthday unguiltily leave his wife. Parents
dead, kids raised, the householder leaves
spouse and home, and goes into the mountains,
where his guru may be. In America, you can yourself
be the guru, *be* the wandering starets.
At his birthday picnic, Wittman Monkey wishes
for that freedom as he and the wind blow out
60-plus candles. Used to telling
his perfectly good wife his every thought,
he anti-proposes to her. "Taña, I love you. But.
I made a wish that we didn't have to be married
anymore. I made a wish for China.
That I go to China on my own." Taña—
beautiful and pretty as always, leaf shadows
rubbing the wrinkles alongside her blue eyes
and her smile, sun haloing her whitegold
hair—Taña lets Wittman's bare words
hang in air. Go ahead, you Monkey.
Wish away. Tell away. Tell it
all away. Then she kicks ass—
"Here's your *one* to grow on!"—then

gets quiet. *She* can be rid of *him*.
But first, have it out. "So, we're not
going to be old lovers, and old artists
together till we die. After all our years
making up love, this thing, love,
peculiar to you and me, you quit,
incomplete. God damn it, Darling,
if your wife—I—were Chinese,
would she be your fit companion in China?"
"Hell, Sweetheart, if you were Chinese,
I wouldn't've married you to begin with.
I spurned the titas for you." Forsaking the sisters.
All my sisters-of-color. O, what

a romance of youth was ours, mating, integrating,
anti-anti-miscegenating. "Bad
Monkey. You married me as a politcal act."
"No, Honey Lamb, uh uh.
An act of artists—the creating of you-and-me."
Married so long, forgot how to declare *I*.
I want Time. I want China.
Married white because whites good at everything.
Everything *here*. Go, live Chinese,
gladly old. America, can't get old,
no place for the old. China, there be

Immortalists. Time moves slower in China.
They love the old in China. No verb
tenses in Chinese, present tense
grammar, always. Time doesn't pass
for speakers of such language. And the poets make
time go backward, write stroke by stroke,
erase one month of age with every poem.

Tuesday, I cried—in public,
a Chinese woman wailing to the streets—
over the headline: LIBBY FINGERS CHENEY.
I'd gloated, but suddenly stopped moving, and wept.

The stupid, the greedy, the cruel, the unfair have taken
over the world. How embarrassing, people asking,
"What's wrong?" and having to answer, "Cheney.
Rumsfeld. Rove. Halliburton. Bush." The liars.
The killers. Taking over the world. Aging,
I don't cry for the personal anymore,
only for the political. Today's news photo:
A 10-year-old boy—his name is
Ali Nasir Jabur—covers his eyes
with his hands. He hunkers in the truck bed
next to the long blanket-wrapped bodies of
his sister, 2 brothers, mother, and father.
A man's bare feet stick out from a blanket

that has been taped around the ankles.

I see this picture, I don't want to live.

I've seen the faces of beaten, cloaked women;

I don't want to live. Their black

wounds are infected, their eyes swollen shut.

Their bodies beaten too, but can't be seen.

I want to lie down and die.

Just last week, 12 sets of bones

from Viet Nam were buried in 12 ceremonies.

At sunset, I join the neighbors—with sangha,

life is worth living—standing at the BART

station, holding lit candles, reminding

one and all that the 2,000th American

soldier has died in Iraq. Not counting

mercenaries, contract workers, Iraqis, Afghanis.

2000X23

The children are quiet. How do their parents

explain war to them? "War." A growl sound.

And the good—capitalistic?—of standing in

the street doing nothing? "People are fighting . . ."

But a "fight" connotes fairness, even-sidedness,

equal powers. ". . . And we're being quiet, thinking

of them, and holding them in our hearts, safe.

We're setting an example of not-fighting.
The cars honking are making good noise;
they're honking Peace, Peace."

                              Wednesday,
birthday eve, I tried re-reading
Don Quixote. (My writings are being translated
into Castellano *and* Catalan. *La Dona Guerrera*.)
The mad and sorry knight is only 50.
Delusions gone, illusions gone, he dies.
Books killed him. Cervantes worked on
Don Quijote de la Mancha while in jail.
For 5 years, he was given solitude,

and paper, ink, and pens, and time. In Chinese
jails, each prisoner is given the 4
valuable things, writes his or her life,
and is rehabilitated. I've been in jail too, but
so much going on, so many
people to socialize with, not a jot
of writing done. The charge against me:
DEMO IN A RESTRICTED ZONE—
WHITE HOUSE SIDEWALK. The U.S.
is turning Chinese, barricading
the White House, Forbidden City, great walls
along the borders.

              Now, it's my birthday.

October 27. And Sylvia Plath's.

And Dylan Thomas's. Once on this date,

I was in Swansea, inside the poet's

writing shed, a staged mess, bottles

and cups on table and floor. A postcard

of Einstein sticking out his tongue.

I like Thoreau's house better, neat and tidy.

I walked out on Three Cliffs Bay.

Whole shells—cockles, mussels, clams,

golden clams, and snails, and oysters, jewels—

bestrew the endless wet land.

I cannot see to the last of it, not a lip of sea.

No surf. "We be surfers in Swansea."

I've never seen tide go out so far.

"The furthest tide in the world." I followed the gleam

of jewels—I was walking on sea bottom—

and walked out and out and out, like the tide

to the Celtic Sea. Until I remembered: the tide

will come back in, in a rush,

and run me down, and drown me. By the time

I see and hear incoming surf,

it will be too late. I ran

back for the seawall, so far away,

and made it, and did not die on that birthday.

Not ready to give myself up.

I have fears on my birthdays. Scared.

I am afraid, and need to write.

Keep this day. Save *this* moment.

Save each scrap of moment; write it down.

Save *this* moment. And *this* one. And *this*.

But I can't go on noting every drip and drop.

I want poetry as it came to my young self

humming and rushing, no patience for

the chapter book.

I'm standing on top of a hill;

I can see everywhichway—

the long way that I came, and the few

places I have yet to go. Treat

my whole life as formally a day.

The light changing as the hours change, the weather

exciting, the weather calming, sunrise

to sunset and the blessed night for sleeping.

I used to be able, in hours, to relive,

to refeel my life from its baby beginnings

all the way to the present. 3 times

I slipped into lives before this one.

I have been a man in China, and a woman

in China, and a woman in the Wild West.

(My college roommate called; she'd met
Earll and me in Atlantis, but I don't
remember that.) I've been married
to Earll for 3 lifetimes, counting
this one. From time to time, we lose each other,
but can't divorce until we get it right.
Love, that is. Get love right. Get
marriage right. Earll won't believe
in reincarnation, and makes fun of it.
The Dalai Lama in *How to Expand Love*
says to try "the possibility that past
and future rebirth over a continuum
of lives may take place." We have forever.

Find me, love me, again.
I find you, I love you, again.
I've tried but could not see
my *next* life. All was immense black
space, no stars. After a while,
no more trying to *pro*gress, I returned—
was returned—to an ordinary scene that happened
yesterday, and every sunny day: Earll and I
are having a glass of wine with supper—bruschetta
from our own tomatoes and basil—under the trellis
of bougainvillea, periwinkly clematis,

and roses. Shadows and sunlight are moving at Indian
summer's pace. The Big Fire burned
the grove of Monterey pines. We planted
purple rain birches, Australian tea
trees, dogwood, the elm, locust, catalpa,
3 redwoods from seed, 4 pepper
willows, and 7 kinds of fruit trees.
The katsura and the yucca are volunteers.
That Texas privet and the bamboo, survivors. Here,
I feel as I felt in Hawai'i, as I felt in Eden.
A joy in place. Adam and Eve were never
thrown out; they grew old in the garden.
They returned after travels. So, I,
like the 14th Dalai Lama, have arrived
at my last incarnation? I don't feel a good
enough person to be allowed off the wheel.
I am guilty for leaving my mother. For leaving
many mothers—nations, my race, the ghetto.
For enjoying unconsciousness and dreams, wanting
sleep like thirst for water. I left MaMa
for Berkeley, then 17 years in Hawai'i.
Couldn't come home winter and spring breaks,
nor summers. She asked, "How can I bear
your leaving?" No, I'm not translating right.

"Can I seh doc your leaving?" Seh doc

tells the pain of losing something valuable.

How can she *afford* my leaving?

Seh doc sounds like *can write*.

Sounds almost like my father's name.

Father who left her behind in China for 15

years. I too left her.

"Lucky," she bade and blessed, in English. "Lucky."

She and Father stood at the gate, looking

after me. Looking after each child as

we left for college, left for Viet Nam.

Her eyes were large and all-holding.

No tears. She only cried when laughing.

Me too. I'm in tears laughing.

From the demimonde, Colette wrote, lying

to her mother, All's well, I'm happy.

Our only son did not leave us;

we left him in Hawai'i.

Generations. Karma. Ah Goong

walked my mother to the end of Tail End

Village. Whenever she looked back, he was still

standing there weeping and looking after her.

I'll watch over Wittman Ah Sing
go through the leaving of his wife. A practicing artist
herself, Taña understands the wanter
of freedom. Let him go. If they stay put,
husband and wife lose each other anyway,
artist and artist dreaming up separate
existences. Go on roads through country you define
as you go. Wend through taboo mazes.
"But, Wittman," says Taña, " 'til death us do part."
(Say those words, and you vow once again.)
"No, Taña, not death, only away awhile."
Married so long, every word and moment is
thick with strata and fathoms and echoes.
35 years ago, they climbed
the Filbert Steps, walked in and out
of garden gates, pretended this house
and that house were home. They'd wed atop
Coit Tower. Look! Where it comes again.
Our wedding tower lifts out of the fog
and the forest edge of the City. "I need
to get to China, and I have to go

without helpmeet. I've been married to you
so long, my world is you. You
see a thing, I see it. The friends you
like, I like. The friends you can't
stand, I can't stand. My
perception is wedded to your perception.
You have artist's eyes. I'd wind up
seeing the China you see. I want
to see for myself my own true China."
Taña says, "So, you don't want to be
with me, and we become old, old
lovers and old artists together. You,
my old lover. I love you, old lover."
Wittman feels a rush that is Taña's benevolence
for him suffuse him. He has to try harder
to leave her. "I love you, Taña. Thank you,
my wife, for our lifetime,
and our past lifetimes. We don't
have to get divorce papers. We quit
being householders is all. The chi
connecting us will stretch infinitely."
On such agreement, the long-married can part.
His birthday morning continues fair. The Bay
is busy with sailboats, and the ocean outside

the Golden Gate calmly opens forever.
All seems well, as though Water Margin
protected us. I have a soul, and it expands large
as I look out at the Pacific; I do
remember to look every single day.
Suddenly, I get scared. Some
fanatic is delivering by freighter or yacht or barge
or cruiser a nuke. BANG! The end.
The separating couple drive to Reno—not
for divorce but to give their son, Mario, a chance
to say Happy Birthday, Dad, and Goodbye.
Spelling each other at the wheel, they cross

stateline at South Shore Lake Tahoe,
travel Highway 50, the Loneliest Road
in America. Objective correlative everywhere—
lonely Sierras, lonely turkey buzzards, lonely
railroad tracks, ghost towns, lone
pines. You can stay on Highway 50
all the way across the U.S.
of A., but they turn off in Reno.
Husband and wife walk its streets hand-in-
hand; they keep ahold of each other;
they could divorce in an instant. They arrive
in the middle of Mario Ah Sing the Real's

Magic Show. (The father a mere monkey,
a trickster; the son a magician of the actual.)
There he is—our dear, only son.
Father and mother feel shock, thrill
at sight of him—grown, a man, a strange-
looking man. It's the Hapa eyes;
he's got the epicanthic fold *and*
the double lid. The better to see you with,
my dear. Mario spots his parents
heading in the dark for the last empty table.
And his patter changes. He is strange-
sounding too, his voice deep even as a
hairy baby. ". . . Raised in Hawai'i, no
picnic. Too much da kine. Da
bad kine. You dink it's all
aloha, you got another dink
coming, Haole. Take dees, Haole.
Take dat, Ho'ohaole." He socks,
he punches, takes socks, takes punches that
clobber him against invisible walls. The audience
laughs. "But. Yet. On the other hand—"
shaking out each sleeve of China Man gown.
Nada up his sleeves. "—the wahine are beautiful.
I love the wahine, and some of them have loved me.

They swam out to meet my ship." He

chants spooky-voice mele, calls

upon his 'aumākua—and a hula girl

appears out of nowhere / somewhere. She

hula hula up to him, her hands

making the " 'ama'ama-come-swimming-to-me"

moves. Mario the Real snags a rope

of flowers in air, raises them above her head,

places them around her neck and shoulders. See?

No strings, no mirrors, no

hologram. Upon being circled, the Little

Brown Gal (in the little grass skirt)

says, "Aloha-a-a, Mario," and on the long

out-breath becomes air. The flower

lei falls to the floor. The audience applauds.

"Aloha to you too," says Mario. "A fine how

do you do. Hello goodbye." He confides

to one and all, strangers and family alike:

"I've just been dumped. My wahine alohaed me.

Auwe! It hurts. Aiya!

My chi is broken. Aiya!" He lifts

his elbows; his arms dangle—broken wings.

The poor parents just about cry.

Oh, our son, our only child hurts

so bad, he presents his pain

for all to see. Oh, the guilt—to've raised

him among Hawai'i's violent people and heart-

breaking girls of every race. "Auwe-e-

e-e. Ai-ya-a-a." And pidgin-speakers

teaching him to howl and yowl and keen. Our fault.

We should've stayed in California, mainland,

home after all. Having a kid

gets you running the hamster wheel.

But the crowd is aiya-ing and auwe-ing.

He has audience; and they're with him, mourning along.

"My penultimate gal, Lori, girlfriend-

before-last, had the ring I gave her assayed.

Assayed?! I'd give her a fake?!

'No, no,' she said, 'not fake.

It's good—twenty-five hundred

dollars. Oh, Mālei. Oh,

Mai'a mālei, I love you.'

No, you don't, Lori. You don't

love me. You had me assayed." The poor

parents should've broken him out of magic.

But he keeps truck with the Little People

(who live in the rocks at the edges of old gardens).

The sharma thrush was his 'aumākua. The pair

that lived in the Surinam cherry hopped in the grass

behind his feet, sang on branches above

his head. All day they sang him night-

ingale songs. All year they flashed him

Hallowe'en colors. Now he plays

clubs and lounges—like night all the time.

Mario the Real uncoils a length of rope.

"This cowboy rope belonged to a paniolo

I rode with on the Big Island. Most likely

any old rope will do.

I throw it into the air like so—and something

or someone catches it. I can feel him or her

or it grab ahold. I better go

exploring, and see . . . " He shinnies up the tense

rope, lifts one foot, sets it down,

then the other, sets it solidly down,

and pulls himself into the invisible.

Mario does not reappear for a curtain call.

The audience waits a stretch of dead time, then

disbands, wanders, examines the rope, which

collapses on the floor, an ordinary thing.

Such relief when the missing son (Oh,

too many dead sons!) in regular

T-shirt and jeans exits the side door
into the parking lot in daylight.
Those who've seen a baby erupt into being
will ever after fear that he'll as suddenly
slide, slip, crash out of life. Now
you see him, now you don't.
Father and mother both have nightmares—
war, the war, the wars happening at this
very instant. A missile drops from the star-
warring sky. A rocket shoots up
out of the mined earth. Harming our child,
who is all the ages he's ever been. Shrapnel
rips through his face, his baby-fat cheeks,
his goateed chin. His mother holds
his head. His father holds his hands—
they've been chopped off. The magician's hands
chopped off. Don't try to comfort me,
that it's only a dream, only a dream.
I answer for what I dream. Kuleana hana.
Our son was born year of the Rabbit.
The character *rabbit* under the character *forest*
under the radical *home* equals the word
magic. It's all right that he didn't graduate
from a 4-year college, didn't become

an engineer. Admire the magician most
of all the artists. He makes something out of
nothing, can himself become nothing.

                    The Ah Sing
family is together again; the parents hug
and kiss their grown son; he hugs and kisses
them back. You are safe. You are safe.
"Happy birthday, Dad. Howzit feel
turning sixty?" The father takes a deep
breath, and answers his son, "Old. I feel
old. I *am* old. No. No.

I don't mean my looks. People of color
revenge: We always look good.
I feel time. It's like a wind
cutting through my skin and insides. When
I was your age, time and I moved
at the same rate. I was *in* time. I went
with the music. The ancestors say: In China,
time moves slow like yearly rice, andante.
Chan / Zen has been working for 2,500
years to stop time—get that now-moment
down. I want to be where no-beginning–
no-end. I'm not good at staying put.

The older I get, the more tripping out
and flashbacks. I live again feelings
I've already gone through. Pink
embarrassments, red guilts, purple guilts.
I see *your* life too. *Your* life flashes
before me. I look at you, my son,
and you are every age. I saw you being
born, face first. I saw your face,
eyes, mouth tight, then maw!
You were mouth, all mouth—red
tunnel into a universe. Then I saw
your whole body, your hairy little wet
body—you were so small, how
can you make your way in the world? How
could I, myself small, safeguard you?
I saw you—I see you—sit up—an owlet
in a nest, blinking big eyes at me, at everything,
ears perky, hair perky. You
were not a cuddle baby. You kicked and punched
out of swaddling, out of diapers, out
of the little gown. You sledded down the stairs
in your walker, bawled at the bottom—alive! You
said, 'My eyes are little, but I can see
so-o-o much!' Your toddling down-

hill faster and faster, and not falling.
Your announcing, 'I am Second Bull
of Second Grade.' Oh, I just now
got it—you were in a fight. You
came out second. I saw you
take your time running the bases—you hit
three men home. Grand slam!
Your popping up out of the ocean—
alive! Rell Sunn the Queen of Makaha
was watching too. Your concentrating for an hour
on the written driver's test. Your telling us that
you obey the law, you registered for the Draft.

I am constantly remembering you." Meaning,
I am constantly *loving* you. I am constantly
worried about you. Old people suffer,
too much feeling, shaking with feeling,
love and grief over too many dear ones,
and rage at all that harms and hurts them.
"Mario, I'm going to China. No,
no, I don't mean I'm going to die there,
home with the ancestors. I'm curious to know
who I am alone among a billion three
hundred million strangers who look like me.
I am Monkey of Changes." Hero of the talk-

stories that he raised his son on.
"I regret I missed the Revolution, and ongoing
revolutions. I was kept busy claiming
this country. 'Love it or leave it.' 'Chink,
go back to China, Chink.' I had to
claim my place, root down, own
America. This land is *my* land.
Why should *we* leave? We who made
everything wonderful, why should *we* leave?"
It's easy to talk yourself out of leaving.
Easier to move in, stay, than to move out, go.

The troops will never come home.

"But now my work establishing Asia America
is done. Our nation won. We have a people.
And passport home. My leaving is not exile.
I must, I need act out my deep
down monkey nature. Wife, son,
let your indulgence set me free."
And so, wife understanding and son
understanding, Wittman Ah Sing
begins his Going Forth. (Buddha left
wife and son. Confucius' wife left him.)

From his bank, the Bank of San Francisco,
China Man took out his money.

Sittin' in the sun,
Countin' my money
Happy as I can be.

How very grand—there's money, money
to spare. Grandparents and parents had had
leftover money too and passed it on.
There's money. Enough to live in a rich country
for 6 months, or in a poor country
for the rest of my life. So-so
Security will send a check every
month to wherever I'll be living.

                              China
begins at the Consulate, where you get your visa.
The last couple of times I, Maxine,
went, members of Falun Gong were protesting
against China persecuting them and their way of
kung fu. At first, they merely moved
and breathed, doing slow, quiet exercises
on the curb in front of the door to the Consulate.
They looked like other Chinatown ladies

who exercise in the parks of San Francisco.
Then, they started showing color photos
of torture—purple black eyes, a red rectum.
Wittman, lover of street theater, come,
talk to them. Three old women meditating
beside their yellow banner with the pink flower.
Look again. The poor things aren't old;
they're younger than oneself. But they dress old,
home-knit vests, home-sewn
pants, the same style patterns passed
along for generations, old country
to new country. They're coifed old-
fashioned, Black Ghost hair.

It is raining. Martyrs praying in the rain,
beseeching China, shame on China. Two
sit cross-legged on the cement, eyes
shut, palms together. The woman who stands
also has her eyes closed; she holds
the banner out from its stanchion, one hand
in prayer position. Bags full of food
to last days. At Tiananmen
Square, the man faced off the tanks
with a bag of groceries in either hand, danced
stepping side to side, tank moving

side to side. A Chinese can dare
anything, do battle, armed with bags of food.
Wittman feels guilty, about to break
his vow never to cross a picket line.
Talk to these women, justify himself.
"Excusu me? Excusu me?" he says
to the woman standing. She opens her eyes,
looking straight at him. "Please, teach me
about Falun Gong." She reaches into a bag,
and gives him a CD, says, "Falun Gong
is good." He goes for his wallet. She waves
No no no—shoos away

payment. Amazing—a Chinese who
doesn't care too much for money.
The label has no info, only
the pink flower logo. "You hear
good. Falun Gong good." "Thank
you. Daw jeah. Jeah jeah. I go
now to apply for visa in-country, your
country, China. I vow, I'll do
something for your freedom of religion. Don't you
worry." "Dui dui dui." I love it
when Chinese make that kind sound.
Dui dui dui. Agree agree agree.

We *conjoin*. *Understand*. We *match*.
(The CD turned out to be blank.
The true scrolls that Tripitaka Tang
and Monkey carried on the Silk Road also blank.
Meaning Noble Silence? Emptiness? Words
no good?) A purer citizen of the world
would boycott China—for tyrannizing Tibet
and Xinjiang, for shooting nuclear missiles
off Taiwan's beam, for making weapons
and selling them to all sides. Better to
communicate or to shun?

                   Inside the Consulate,
the Chinese diaspora are seeking permission
home, yelling its dialects and languages,
the Cantonese hooting, honking like French,
lisping like Spaniards, aiya-ing, the northerners
shur-shur-shurring. We're nervous.
The borders are sealed, the homelands secure.
Every nation state is mean with visas.
Especially the U.S.A., especially
the P.R.C. We shut
them out, they shut us out.
Even Canada, even Mexico.
(But here's a deal, brokered by our office

of Homeland Security: 39,000

visas back to China for aliens and/or

refugees. Can you trust that?)

Wait in line at the Applications window,

come back next week to Payment,

then Pick Up. In plain sight is money

heaped on a table, piles of banded bills

and loose bills. We're the rich; we saved up

for years, for lifetimes, able to afford

travel to the other side of the world.

The form asks for one's "Chinese name."

At last, I've got a use for the Chinese name.

Space to write it 2 different ways:

characters and alphabet.

Hong Ting Ting. The poet Liu Shahe,

who sings Walt Whitman, sang my name,

"Tong Ting Ting, the sound of pearls,

big pearl and little pearls falling

into a jade bowl bell." His fingers formed

pearls and dropped them into his cupped hand.

Now Wittman writes his Chinese name:

Chung Fu. Center Truth. When I first

imagined him, I gave him that name

as a brother name to my son's,

Chung Mei. Center Beauty. My son,

child of Center Nation and Beautiful Nation.

Hexagram 61 of the I Ching

is Chung Fu, Center Truth. Don't

believe those who tell you Chinese

have no word for *truth*. (Ha Jin

told me "we" have no word for *truth*,

nor *privacy*, nor *identity*.) Truth's pictograph

is the claw radical over the child radical.

Americans understand, eagle snatches

Truth in talons. But to the Chinese,

the brooding mothering bird's feet gently

hold the hatchling's head. A cap of eggshell

clings to baby Truthie's fontanel.

The superior person broods the truth. And if

his words are well spoken, he meets with assent—

dui dui dui dui—at a distance

of more than 1,000 miles. We won our visas.

Our names are legal, and we win countries.

Though we Chinese and we Americans

shouldn't need passports and visas

to cross each other's borders and territories.

President Grant and Emperor Tongzhi

signed a treaty giving freedom of travel—

"for purposes of curiosity, of trade, or
as permanent residents." The right to curiosity!
Curious Monkey waves the Burlingame Treaty
under the noses of officials at every checkpoint,
and is let through. I, though, am nervous
at Passport Control. When I was arrested
for demonstrating at the White House, I couldn't
find my I.D., couldn't be booked
properly. "Overnight in the big cell
for *you* tonight." I phoned Earll in California.
He tore the cover off my passport,
and fed it through the fax. I watched
the copy arrive at Federal prison—an illegible
dark zigzag mackle. I've glued
the little book back together along
its stitched spine. Crossing any border,
I'm nervous, it'll fall apart. I'm nervous,
I have relatives in China. My actions and words
can endanger them. And I have relatives who
work at the Lawrence Livermore Laboratory;
you lose your job if you have foreign family.

Wittman is all-American; no
relatives anywhere but the U.S.A.

Goodbye, Husband. Goodbye,
Wife of almost all my life.
Goodbye, my one and only child.
Now, they are in my arms.
Now, I turn, they go. Zaijian.
Joy kin. Ropes, veins, hairs
of chi that root the leaver to home pull,
stretch, attenuate as we move apart.
The red string—I can feel it. Can't
you feel it?—has tied us espoused ones
ankle to ankle since before we met,
before we were born, and will connect
us always, and will help us not to miss
each other too much. Westward East.

Facing west from California's shores,
Inquiring, tireless, seeking what is yet unfound,
I, a child, very old, over waves, toward the house of
      maternity, the land of migrations, look afar,
Look off the shores of my Western sea, the circle
      almost circled . . .

Wittman is going to China for the first time.
I have been 12 times, counting

Hong Kong and Taiwan as China.

Long having wander'd since—round the earth having
   wander'd.
Now I face home again—very pleas'd and joyous.
(But where is what I started for so long ago?
And why is it yet unfound?)

But I did not wander, never
wandered, and never alone. I have responsible
work to do, the teaching, the writing. I
am writing right now on an airplane,
above thick clouds. I've taken the window seat.
Upon the dragon clouds, Mother's soul
walks toward Father's soul. He's holding open
a shawl; he's hugging her in it. They're happy,
they're home, ancestors all around.
The clouds dispel. Ocean and sky on and
on and on. Land. Mountains. Circles
of irrigated fields, squares of plowed
fields. From on high, human beings
and all the terrible things they do and make
are beautiful. Loft your point of view above
the crowd, the party, any fray. All

is well. All always well. Land,
Chek Lap Kok International. Hong Kong.
The soldiers at Passport Control do not
say Aloha, welcome, dear traveller, welcome.
But then, no such hospitableness anymore
at any border-crossing on earth. (Once,
at the supermarket in Ann Arbor, in America's
Heartland, the butcher called out
to an Asian-looking man and woman, "Where
you from?" The man of the couple answered, "Seoul,
Korea." The butcher said, "Welcome, sir. Ma'am.
Welcome to Michigan.") Wittman took the train,
got off in Central, and alighted tomorrow in the Land
of Women. Women everywhere—the streets, the parks,
the alleys, the middle of streets. All the city
was closed today, Sunday. Women on sidewalks,
curbs, stairs up and down hills—
everywhere women. Women of his very
type, beauties with long black hair
gathered up or cascading down,
naturally tan skin, dark eyes
the warmest brown, lashes like black fans.
The women were of one generation—no matrons,
no little girls, no crones.

Thala-a thala-a-a. The one
man, knapsack on his back,
stepped—delighted, curious, englamoured, happy—
among, around women. Women picnicking,
drinking sodas and juices. Women
playing cards. Women combing and trimming
their sisters' hair. Painting emblems and charms
on fingernails and toenails. A solitary
is reading a book. Another writing a letter.
Mostly the women converse. The sound of their language
is like hens cluck-clucking. They talk, talk,
listen, listen, listen. For them, the city

stilled. Women walked and lingered on streets
meant for cars. What are they saying about life,
about love, these Peripatetics from the Pilippines?
Wittman circled este grupo, ese
grupo. No woman paid him look
or heed. Standing on a box in an intersection,
a sister raised Bible and voice to the crowd
and/or to God. Sisters (and brother
Wittman) tarried and stared, then floated away
on the wavery heat of the tropical sun. They passed
expensive stores, passed luxury hotels—
five stars all. (My mother

on her way to catch the S.S. *Taft,*
fled the police soldiers by running inside
one of these hotels.) A bronze sign on
a movable stand placed mid-sidewalk
says:

IN CONSIDERATION FOR HOTEL GUESTS,

PLEASE DO NOT BLOCK

ENTRANCEWAY.

The women sat at the curb, like hippies.
Free of husband, free of kids. Like
on vacation abroad with girlfriends.
Oh, let me be hippie with you.
Just like we were last summer!
The women and the hotel people act as if
the other did not exist. A vendor of sweets,
a man, set his wagon down; the women
crowded, haggling, selecting, buying just
the right treat—that candy for me,
that cookie for best girlfriend.
All people smile and laugh when anticipating
dessert. Along another curb, a row of
women stood in political demonstration.

They'd appliquéd a paragraph on a long
piece of cloth. Something about la inmigración.
Something something derechos. Rights.
Los derechos de criadas.
"What is criadas?" asked Wittman.
"Maids. Servants. Maids." So, these masses
of women are maidservants, and today their day
off, Sunday. And they want their rights.
Tell them, Wittman: "In San Francisco,
we have inmigrante workers too.
We want los derechos too."
"O-o-oh, San Francisco," breathe

the women, "O-o-oh, California."
They like you from San Francisco, and California,
my places, and Hawai'i, and the Grand Canyon,
also my places. I have places the world
dreams for, hardly knowing they're U.S.
"Are you organizing
las criadas labor union? Los
Commies allow unions? Commies have servants?"
A sassy girl waved a handful of papers.
"We want long long stay bisas
for Pilipina maids." I get it: visas.
"To stay, to work. For Hong Kong to be

safe harbor. We want health
insurance." "We too. We want
health insurance too. Universal
human derecho." Simpático. The women told
the man their grievances: "The bishop's Pilipina
maid cooked and cleaned house for eighteen
years. She grew old, and is sick in hospital.
The Chinese will deport her."
Yes, Hispanics like you get deported
in my country too. Operation Return
to Sender. "The bishop went to the bisa office,
petition for her, his housekeeper. Chinese
ask, 'She fit or not fit for work?'
Can't work, must deport.
That's all Hong Kongers care."
"The other day, a maid fell four
stories. From up there—that high
up. Madam made her wash the windows.
She's alive. She's in hospital, but who
will pay? Who will send money
to her husband and babies?" Wittman could pay.
Pay for the hospital, pay for the babies, pay
for the whole village. Rich American karma:
Pay. Pay. Pay. (*Karma* is Sanskrit

for *work. Karma* does not mean *doomed.*
All it means: *work.*) From a pocket of his Levi's,
he pulled out the U.S.D.s and the R.M.B.s.
"Here. Yes, yes. Take it. Please.
For you. All yours." He's got more;
he's got enough. "Give it to the bishop's house-
keeper. Give it to the window-washer maid."
Giving away money, don't make
the donee feel poor, and don't you
be her fish. Our donator finessed
the bills under a brick that held flyers
down. "Use it to lobby for health and visas.

Thank you for taking care of citizen business
though not citizens. No, no problem.
Thank *you.* Goodbye."
                              Behind the great
windows of the Bank of China (Hong Kong)—
open but not for business—a priest
in white and gold regalia was lifting a chalice—
not toward any altar, his back to the congregants
(as in Earll's day), but toward Pilipina maids.
Pilipina maids knelt and sat on
the marble floor, scarved heads bowed
and palms together, attitudes so humble,

you could cry. They give in, they *thank*.
Old Monkey would've jumped into the crowd,
snatched wine and mitre, slurped up the wine,
donned the hat, pissed in the cup. Today
Monkey went quiet. Quiet prevailed.
He backed out of the bank that's church this Sunday,
and continued his walkabout basking in the alma
and the mana of Yin. In a bright alley, jam-
packed with boxes, mothers and godmothers
filled cartons with toys and dried milk
and canned milk, and children's clothes and shoes,
and men's clothes and shoes. Las madres y
las comadres shared tape, string, scissors,
and wrote out postal and customs forms.
They are saviors of families, villages, populations.
Woman's adventure, woman's mission.
The lone male looking at them was no bother.
But they hated *me*, a woman, seeing them.
They looked back at me, shot me with hate.
Turned to follow me with their eyes, hate
firing from their eyes. They hated me.
Hate-stares followed me though I walked
with the attitude that I was at home among my own
Asian sisters. In words, they'd be calling me

names. "You fucking bitch empress. You

make me clean your toilet. You make me sleep

in the toilet." Though catching stinkeye,

a curling lip, a dissing shrug of shoulders,

I willed a kind and pleasant mien.

May you be happy, you be safe.

May you make much, much money.

May your children and family be happy and safe,

and you return home to them soon.

I must remind them of Madam, their Chinese employer.

But I don't look like a Chinese matron.

I don't dye my hair black. I'm not

wearing my gold and jade. They don't know

I bought these clothes at the Goodwill.

I'm wearing shoes donated after the Big Fire.

They don't know, most of my nieces and nephews

are Filipino, and 9 great-nieces

and great-nephews, Filipino Chinese

Americans. They don't know me, I am like them,

my marriage like theirs. Wife works for money;

husband, employed or unemployed, has fun.

Son, too, has fun. Men know how

to play. Music. Sports. Theater. These women

don't know, I work 2 jobs.

I moonlight, do the work-for-money
and the writing. I wish I
had thought to be a stay-at-home mom.
(How interesting: The girl makes wishes for
the future. The eldress, for the past.)
I, too, send money to villages, the promise
made to family when leaving them. My BaBa,
who arrived in New York City when Lindberg
landed in Paris, vowed: I will not
forget you. I will always send money
home. The Pilipina maids see
me a lazy dowager, and hate me.
Crone. Witch. Aswang. Old woman
going about with long hair down
like a young woman's, but white. Normal
in Berkeley, beautiful in Berkeley. And in the Philippines
I'm already in costume for Aswang Festival,
day before Hallowe'en, days after
my birthday. Come on, fête me and my season.

On the grass in a city park, our male traveller
feeling his lone hobo self, laid
his body down with backpack for pillow.
In San Francisco, it was 2 o'clock the night

before. Going west from California's
shores, jumping forward in time, he'd arrived
at the house of maternity, the land of migrations.
Sleeping in public, jet-lagged, soul
not caught up with body, body
loose from soul, body trusted itself to
the grass, the ground, the earth, the good earth,
and rested in that state where dream is wake,
wake is dream. Conscious you are conscious.
Climb—fly—high and higher, and know:
Now / Always, all connects to all.
All that is is good. His ancestresses—

PoPo Grandma and Ma,
so long in America—are here, the Center.
Expired, Chinese people leave go of
cloudsouls that fly to this place.
Breathe, and be breathed. The air smells
of farawayness. Seas. Trash. Old
fish. The Chinese enjoy this smell,
fragrant, the *hong* in Hong Kong, Fragrant Harbor.
Yes, something large, dark, quiet,
receptive—Yin—is breathing, breathing me
as I am breathing her. My individual
mind, body, cloudsoul melds

with the Yin. Mother. I'm home. But
stir, and the Land of Women goes. Wittman
arose to bass drums of engines—multiple
pulses and earth-deep throbs. Forces
of rushing people. Monday morning go-
to-work people. The City. (The late riser
has missed the tai chi, the kung fu,
the chi kung. While he was sleeping, the artists
of the chi, mostly women, Chinese
women, were moving, dancing the air / the wind /
energy / life, and getting the world turning.
They'd segued from pose to pose—spread
white-crane wings, repulse monkey,
grasp bird by tail, high pat
on horse, stand like rooster on one leg,
snake-creep down, return to mountain.
They played with the chi, drawing circles in the sky,
lifting earth to sky, pulling sky
to earth, swirling the controllable universe.
Then walked off to do their daily ordinary tasks.)
Wittman, non-moneymaker, fled
the financial district. Already dressed,
the same clothes asleep and awake, he merged
with a crowdstream, and boarded a westbound

train. Go deep in-country.

Find China. Hong Kong is not China.

The flow of crowd stopped, jammed inside

the train. Wittman was one among the mass

that shoved and was shoved onto the area

over the coupling between cars. They

would ride standing pressed, squashed,

breathing one another's breath, hoisting

and holding loads—Panasonic and Sony

ACs—above heads. The train

started, the crowd lurched, the air conditioners

rocked, almost fell but didn't. Men

prized through the packed-tight crowd,

squeezed themselves from one car to the next,

and back again. A man, not a vendor,

jostled through, lugging a clinking

weight of bottled drinks that could've smashed

the upturned faces of the short people. Bags

smelled of cooked meat. I have food,

I can do anything. I know I can.

I know I can. Hard-seat travel.

Suffer more, worth more. The destination

more worth it. The Chinese have not

invented comfort. People fell asleep

on their feet. They work hard, they're tired,
grateful for a spot of room to rest. Rest.
Rest. A boy slept astraddle his father,
father asleep too, 2 sleeping
heads, head at peace against head.
Had Wittman and his son ever shared one
undistracted moment of being quiet?
Though tall, he could not see above the crowd
and their belongings. What country was rolling past
unappreciated? The train—a local—made stops.
More people squeezed aboard. On and on
and on, yet on the border of immense China.
You've heard, always heard: China's
changing. China's changed. China gone.
Old China nevermore. Too late.
Too late. Too late. Too late.
Voyage far, and end up at another
globalized city just like the one you left.
Vow not to stop until you can alight
in green country. Country, please remain.
Villages, remain. Languages, remain.
Civilizations, remain. Each village
a peculiar civilization. The mosh between
cars did empty. You got to sit

in the seat you'd paid for. Hillsides
streaming by on the north; on the south,
a river. Arched doors built into
slopes of hills. Cry "Open sesame!"
and enter the good earth. People walking
the wide, pathless ground, placing on the thresholds
flowers and red paper, wine and food,
incense. Ah, altars, doorsills of graves.
Ah, Ching Ming. All over China,
and places where Chinese are, populations
are on the move, going home. That home
where Mother and Father are buried. Doors
between heaven and earth open wide.
Our dead throng across the bourn,
come back to meet us, eat and drink with us,
receive our gifts, and give us gifts.
Listen for, and hear them; they're listening for
and hear us. Serve the ancestors come back
to visit. Serve them real goods. If
no real goods, give symbols.
Enjoy, dear guests, enjoy life again.
Read the poems rising in smoke. Rituals
for the dead continue, though Communist Revolution,
Cultural Revolution, though diaspora. These hills

could be the Altamont Pass, and the Coast Range
and Sierras that bound the Central Valley. I
have arrived in China at the right time, to catch
the hills green.

               And where shall I be buried?
In the Chinese Cemetery on I-5?
Will they allow my white spouse? We integrate
the cemetery with our dead bodies? It's been my
embarrassing task to integrate social functions.
Can't even rest at the end. Where
Father and Mother are buried, at the Hong gravestone.
Cremate me then. Burn me to ashes. Dig me into
the peat dirt of the San Joaquin Valley.
Dig some more of me into the 'aina of Hawai'i.
Leftovers into the sipapu
navel at the bottom of the Grand Canyon, and more
leftovers at the feet of oaks in Oakland
and redwoods in Muir Woods and eucalyptus
in the Berkeley grove, and around Shakespeare's
plants in Golden Gate Park. All my places.
Yosemite. The Sierras. A few handfuls of me
off the Golden Gate Bridge, which I bladed across.
And my last ashes on Angel Island, where
my mother was jailed on her way to my father and America.

Thinking about death and far from home, Wittman,

a skinny old guy with nothing to eat, looked

lonely. Chinese cannot bear

anyone being lonely. Loneliness is torture.

(What's the word for *lonely*? "Nobody," they say.

"I have nobody.") Passengers this side and that side

proffered food. Buns, *bow*. Pickled

vegetables. Candied vegetables. Chicken fingers.

Beef jerky. They said, Eat, la. Eat, la.

Chinese can't eat unless everybody eats.

"Daw jay," he said, "Dough zheh. Jeah jeah.

Je je nay. Je je nee."

Thanking in variations of accents and tones.

An old lady (that is, a person

of his own age), wiped the rim of her vacuum

bottle cup, poured, and with both hands

handed him tea while saying, "Ngum cha.

Ngum, la." Being given tea,

accepting tea, you drink humbly, but think:

I am being welcomed, honored, adored. Out of all

who exist, we 2 tea drinkers

together. Be ceremonial and mindful, we

are performing Tea, performing the moment of eternity.
The tea woman, in the facing seat, held
a box in her lap. The size of a head.
The Man Who Would Be King's head.
Pointing with his chin as Chinese do,
Wittman impolitely asked, "What
do you have in there?" Can't be nice with small
vocabulary. She answered, or he understood
her to answer: "I'm a-train-riding
with my husband, carrying my old man home,
ashes and smashed bones." "Aiya! How did he die?"
"Martial arts killed him." Or "Bitter work
killed him." Kung fu. Kung *fu.*
"Aiya-a-a," chorused the Big Family.
Everyone listening, the widow told her life.
It went something like this: "Not so
long ago, a *loon* time, an era
of *loon,* this man, this very
man now ashes and bones, swam at night
from China to Hong Kong. A boat family,
who harbored in the Typhoon Shelter, gave
him bed on the water, and shared him 2 meals.
Day, they rowed him to a station for signing up
to live in a safe place / haven / sanctuary /

refugee camp. I.I." Illegal Immigration.

"Aiya-a-a." "O, Big Family,

hear me. For *loon* years, he—I too—

I was I.I. too—lived

up on top of the barbwired hill.

We met at the fence at the farthest edge. He

looked off the shores toward his lost country.

I looked off toward *my* lost country.

His was that dark mass that looms right there

forever across the Straits. Han Mountain.

He'd say, 'They can see us. They can see us better

than we can see them.' Hong Kongers

are rich, they waste money on electricity,

keep lights open all night long.

I could not see *my* country, Viet Nam.

Too far, and China in the way.

We married. We wrote: 'We marry.

Free or in prison, forever, we marry.'

If only we could write 'legal immigrants,'

and be legal immigrants."

                    Why always

Illegal Immigration? Oh, no one

ought be made alien to any country.

No more borders. Nosotros no

cruzamos la frontera; la frontera
nos cruza.

        The Vietnamese Chinese
woman addressed tout le monde, including
her husband, a ghost, who was standing behind
Wittman. He was a ghost in the listening crowd,
and he was the ashes and bones in the box.
"You were a good man, Old Rooster.
You worked hard. A farmer works hard.
He'll always work hard, his life hard,
though he leaves the farm. Though farm /
ground / earth / floor be taken from him."
The chorus intoned: "Aiya. Hai, la."
"Taken by the government." "Taken by business."
"Taken by brothers." "Deem the land." "One
day mid-harvest, a middling harvest,
you, Old Rooster, gave up the fields,
and went to 'seek your fortune.'" She said
in English, "seek your fortune." A generation
had learned the language from fairy tales broad-
cast by loudspeakers across the commune
agricultural zone, across orchards,
furrows, paddies, dairies. "Farewell,
dear Father. Farewell, dear Mother.

The open road beckons me." "Farewell,
my child. Go forth. Win your fortune.
Make money, my son. Find love.
Marry the princess." The widow spoke addressing
her husband, telling him his own story.
"Following the waterways, you walked and swam,
swam and walked from duck pond and streams
and rivers to the Mouth of the Tiger. You had no
Permit To Settle. All through nights,
lights beckon Hong Kong Hong Kong
red red green green. Liang
liang. Ho liang. You swam

for those lights, and came to the ten thousand
sampans, the floating town gone now.
Free and safe for a night and a morning. Boat
people fed you and let you sleep, gave you
bed on the water, fed you twice, supper
and breakfast. JAWK!" She hit the box, caged
it with fingers and arms. "They CAUGHT him."
Wittman jumped. She laughed; everybody
laughed. "Don't be scared, foreign
Chinese person. They did not
torture my husband to death. He got
hit a few times was all. You know

the Chinese, they hit to teach you a lesson.
I saved him out of I.I. I got
out of jail because China and Viet Nam
became normal. Han and Viet same-same."
"Hai, law. Hai, law." Her American
listener chimed in: "Hola! Hola!
In California, we, Chinese and
Vietnamese, together celebrate Tet."
Sing dawn. Tet nguyen dân.
"I took you, my Chinese husband, by the hand,
and we left prison. I'm the one,
freed you, you Old Rooster. Woman
is better at living than man is. We
went to live in public housing just
like everybody else, the sampan
people, everybody. I made
money. All I do, each meal,
I cook enough for more than 2—
2 people eat very little.
The extra, I sell on the street. A hungry man
always comes along; he'll buy
breakfast or lunch or dinner or suey yeah.
Life is easier on a woman. Your abilities,
my good Old Rooster, were to swim and to farm.

In the city, you had to sell your *lick*.
Ladies and gentlemen fellow travelers, he
sold his kung." His strength, his labor. "You
rode a water-soldier boat out
to one of the warships from all over
the world. I watched you be lifted and lowered
by ropes. You hung from ropes down the side
of the ship's mountainface. Using rags,
you painted the gray ship gray,
ashes, ashes, gray on top of gray.
Fields of gray above you and behind you, you
and the cadre of painters—many women—women,
who adore flowers—oozed gray everywhere
you touched. Metal doubled the sun's heat,
and baked you, baked lead paint into
your skin. You could've let yourself
fall backward into air and water. But you,
everyday you went to Pun Shan Shek
and toiled for me. For me, you caught yang
fever. You breathed poison. Skin and lungs
breathed poison, sweated poison. We
could not wash the gray paint out of you.
It was painting warships killed you. That work
so dangerous, the foreign nations don't order

their own water soldiers to do it. Old One,
I thank you for your care of me. You are / were
a good hardworking husband to me.
I'm sorry / I can't face you, my gray
Old Rooster, we never had a son.
Okay. We're each other's child.
I take care of you, and you take care of me.
I bring you home. I'm sorry / I can't
face you, I have taken too long
to bring you home. Stacks and stacks of caskets
and urns wait to get out of Hong Kong.
I pulled you out of the pile-up. We're on
our way home. You're a good man.
You worked hard. Jeah jeah jeah.
Daw jeah. Thanks thanks thanks.
Big thanks." No verb tenses,
what is still happening? What is over?
Yet refugee camps? Yet piles
of unburied dead? Yet coolies painting
ships with lead? All that's happened always
happening? "I too am walking mountain,"
said a man dressed Hong Kong styly,
expensive suit, expensive shoes, expensive
luggage. "I'll sweep the graves, I mean, fix them.

Find my people's bones, and bury them again."
(Oh, to say "my people.") "Cousin
was mad; he dug up Po and Goong."
Mr. Walking Mountain laughed—heh
heh heh heh. Chinese laugh
when telling awfulness. "Cousin dug and cried,
dug and cried, 'Out the Olds! Out
the Olds! Out! Out, old family.
Out, old thoughts. Out! Out!'
He dug up our grandparents and scattered
their bones—ha ha ha—because
I was rich in Hong Kong and did not
send money—heh heh heh—
did not feed him, did not make good,
did not make good him." Chinese
laugh when pained. "I return. I shall
walk mountain, and follow li. I'll
make good the ancestors." *Jing ho.*
Make good. Fix. "Dui dui,"
said the Big Family. "Dui dui dui."
Oh, to hear dui dui dui
to whatever I have to say.
The listening world gives approval, dui
dui dui dui. The train stops

at stations in built-up places. Where's
open country? The planted fields, water
and rice, rice and water, are but green
belts around factory-villages. Those are
50-gallon drums of something rusting
into the paddy. That apartment and that
factory *is* a village. Legs of Robotron
stomp through the remains of the old pueblo.
Gray pearlescence—marshes and lakes,
mists and skies mirroring mirroring. Beautiful,
and alive. Or dead with oil slick? Mist
or smoke? Why are Wittman and I
on journey with the dead, and escorts of the dead?
Toward sunset, there swung past
a series of pretty villages, yellow adobe
houses, almost gold in the last light,
almost houseboats, wood railings
on the river for laundry and fishing. Half
the homes hung on either bank. Make
up your mind, Monkey, get off the train,
see the rivertown, enter its symmetry.
Paddle that river straight down the valley;
stream with the sun's long rays. Walk
the right bank and the left bank. Get

yourself invited into those homes. Sit
on the balcony facing the river and the neighbors
on the other side, everyone's backs to mountains.
Upon Good Earth, lay the body down,
open the mouth wide, let song rush through.

RICE VILLAGE

At the next station, Wittman, nobody else,
got off. The moment his feet touched ground,
the Chinese earth drew him down
to her, made him fall to his knees, kowtow
and kiss her. Gravity is love force. It bends
light and time and us. Mother pulls us to
her by heart roots. I have felt Great Spirit
before: Touching the green wood door
of Canterbury Cathedral. Hearing the air
of Hawai'i sing, 'Aina. Standing in the fire
zone, where my house and neighborhood were burning.
Lofting great balls of pink mana
at the White House and Bush, and Iraq.
The interested traveller walked along the railroad
tracks, then up on path atop bunds.

In the San Joaquin Delta, we walk and run
and bicycle upon dikes too, call them levees.
Many kinds of plants. Crop diversity.
Rice in all stages of growing and going
to seed. All seasons happening at once.
Plains and terraces, levels and hills, greens
dark and light, blues, and straw, are dotted
with moving red—the farmers are working dressed
in red. They can see where one another are.
They are seen; they are lucky. It's beautiful
and lucky to dot red on anything—cookies,
buns, baby carriers, envelopes, white
chicken meat, white dogs. On one's self,
who blesses the earth good and red.

Wittman got to their village before they did,
nightfall ere home from work. The yellow
adobe pueblo was one conjoined structure.
Neighbor and neighbor lived with common walls
this side and that side. Each life impacts
every life. You'd have to live carefully.
You'd watch your moods. And your actions.
Curious Monkey entered through an opening
in a wall and faced another wall,

decided to go right, right being
the right way, usually. The next doorway
took him to an alley; he could look-see
into courtyards, like outdoor kitchens
and laundries and pantries and even bedrooms.
An old squatting grandma was stirring a wok.
Another was washing vegetables. They paid no
mind to the stranger shadowing by. Kitty
cats and a big pig and chickens—swine flu,
bird flu—slinked, lumbered, scratched,
came and went into and out of houses.
That alley jigjagged into another

alley that opened on to the public square.
La plaza at the center of the pueblo. And at the center
of the plaza was the waterworks, not a fountain
but two porcelain troughs with PVC
pipes above and below, and faucets in rows.
Cupping water in worship-like hands
(turn off tap with elbow), quaff
as if welcoming myself with ceremony,
joining myself to this place. Drinking,
aware that I, a citizen from the wealthiest,
squanderingest country, am taking precious water.
Unpurified tap water. Aware that I

risk my life, I throw in my lot
with the health of this common village. Sit
right down on the curbstone on the east
side of the square. Face the last of the sun.
Unpack notebook and pen. Write:

> arrive
> adobe
> China
> home

At home in a civilization kind with plazas,
containing me and the sky and a square of earth.

> Father Sky
> Mother Earth

It's not only Native Americans who pray
Father Sky Mother Earth. Chinese
say Father Sky Mother Earth too.
In the almanac of stars, moons, luck, and farming:

 Ba

T'ien

Ma

Day

Doff sneakers, doff socks, feel
the ground with naked soles. The floor of the plaza
is warm and smooth; skin meets skin.
Chinese generations walked
barefoot here, sweated, oiled,
spat upon, tamped the black soil,
which they could've planted, so rich. Now,
the farmers, men and women, homeward plod.
A goatherd following his goats and sheep,
a duckherd his ducks, light and long shadows
of many legs oscillating. They came upon
the writing man—poet!? retired philosopher!?—
in the act of public writing. Quietly,
they peered over his shoulders, peered over
his right (writing) hand, peered over
his other hand. By calligraphy, they can tell
character and fate. Readers jostled

one another for the spot directly in front,
looked at his writing upside down,
craned their necks to see it from his point
of view. English! The Brave Language. But
his Chinese! A boy's Chinese.
The man draws like a boy. "Read, la.
Read, la-a." Our not-so-ugly American
dared recite loudly, in his best language
and second-best language, the 4-word
poems. Audience clapped hands, and laughed,
and mimicked, and asked, "You've come from what
far place, aw?" "I was born in the Beautiful
Country." "Aiya-a. Beautiful Country.
Is Beautiful Country truly beautiful and rich?"
"Well . . ." (*Well,* English, American.) "Beautiful
Country People are like me, not too
beautiful, not too ugly, not too
rich, not too poor. But some
too rich, too poor. Most,
my color skin, tan. Our color
skin." Actually, the color skin of the people
around was darker, darker from working in the sun.
"I live in Big City. Eighty
out of one hundred people live in the cities.

But I am not like everybody.

Everybody has cars. 2 cars.

I don't have one car.

I don't want one car."

Have and *want,* same sound, not

same tone. They pitied him, poor man,

no car. Audience grew, 50

souls hearing the sojourner who'd seen the Beautiful

Country, who'd learned to write their horizontal alphabet.

People vied with one another, please,

dear writer traveller teacher, come

to our home for eat-rice, and stay the night.

A confident village, the people not shy

to bring you home and see their hovel.

He chose a solid-seeming man, mine

good host, and comradely put himself in yoke.

The farmers, washing up in public, showed off

the on-and-off faucets and the pipes. They filled

wood buckets and plastic buckets and jars.

Wittman asked for a carrying pole across

his neck, above his backpack, which steadied

and cushioned the bouncy, springy, sloshing, heavy

double load. Proudly, he sidestepped

through alleyways and around corners, and up and over

the raised threshold into the courtyard,

brought that water home where he would stay.

His host—Lai Lu Gaw,

Brother Lai Lu—praised and thanked

Witt Man Gaw—shouted, "A good person

has come to visit us!" Out of the dark

of an open doorway appeared a woman. How

to describe Beauty? Perfection. Symmetry. Beyond

compare in all aspects—intelligence of gaze,

tallness of stature, star presence, gentilesse.

Not young, not old. Just right.

What a good man am I, able

to love looks so not-American. Bro

Lai Lu introduced her as Moy Moy.

Younger Sister. (Lower tone: Plum Plum.)

They're not husband and wife. Father and daughter?

Brother bade brother, Come in,

la. Sit, la. Rest, la.

Home, la. The men sat on stools

at a low table. The woman brought tea;

she poured. With both hands, she

held the cup out to the guest, who

quickly accepted it with his 2 hands.

I am paying you my full attention.

The Communists and the Cultural Revolution have not
wiped out manners. Hosts and guest drank
without speaking. From the dark loft hung,
high and low, dried and drying plants,
tree branches, gourds with writing on them, clusters
of seeds, baskets. On the ground, the dirt floor,
all around were open jars and sealed
jars, bales, bundles, sheaves. We
are bowered in a nest. Smell: medicine herbs,
chrysanthemum, mustard, licorice, cilantro,
vinegar. The poor save everything, all
they make and grow, and so feel abundant.
Please don't want to be like us. Don't want.
Host as well as hostess carried from stove
and cooler, from pots and jars, dishes of brown
foods. A cauldron of white rice, enough
for meal after meal. The brown foods
tasted like jerked meat, sausage, brined
and sugared citrus and plums. Moy Moy
got up, and cooked afresh peas and choy,
greens of the new harvest. Back-home
Chinese, too, cook throughout
the dinner party, everybody in
the kitchen. The hostess began conversation:

"Are you married?" What answer but Yes?
"Yes. She's not Chinese." Too
small vocabulary, blurt it all. "She's
white ghost woman. Her name, Taña,
means Play." (*Fawn*. Lower tone: *Food*.)
"I married Play. Heh heh.
I married Food. She married me.
I am with her more years than I am without her."
Hard to parley verb tenses. And don't want
to admit: Marry white, escape karma.
"How much money did you pay
for your airplane ticket?" She's rude, bad
manners East and West to ask cost.

Truth-caring Wittman answered, "One
thousand dollars one-way." Impossible
to explain redeeming coupons, miles, life
savings. "Waaah! One thousand dollars!?!
What do you do to make such money?"
"I write." Impossible to explain the life
in theater. The moneymaking wife. "So,
how do *you* make *your* money?" "Farmer
peasants don't make money, don't
use cash." They live as most human
beings have lived, directly on ground that gives

work and sustenance. "Mr. American Teacher,
will you marry me, and get me out
of the countryside?" "But I'm already married.
I have a wife and son." "No matter.
No problem. Marry me, a Chinese
woman. Chinese women are beautiful,
kind, and good." "I came but today to the country-
side, and do not want to leave it."
The brother spoke up, "I want to
stay in the countryside too. I learned
the lesson Chairman Mao sent us down
to learn: People who work earth know
true good life." "Where were you
sent down from?" "Shanghai City."
The Shanghainese took the worst
punishment in the 10 Years of Great Calamity.
"We read. Both of us, readers. So sent
down, Moy Moy to Xinjiang,
I to another part of Xinjiang,
far far west, beyond Xizang,
almost beyond China. There are Uighur
Chinese, Muslim Chinese,
Xizang Chinese. The women—
they're so free—whirl and twirl,

raise their arms to the sky. The music comes
from bagpipes. Pairs of women lift and
lower the grain pounder—bang bang bang bang—
a music too. Their religion has to do with
buffalos. They collect the skulls and long horns,
and put them on a wall or on the floor,
and that place changes to a holy place.
That area was made good. I felt
the good. I am able to know Good."
So, what does Good feel like?
He could not say. Or he did say,
but in philosopher's language, and my Chinese
not good enough to hear. "After

Great Calamity, after Xinjiang,
I went on the road. People are still
on the road, millions traveling like
desert people. But the desert people
go on roads they know for ten
thousand years. We seek work.
We seek justice." Or *restitution*.
Or *revenge. Come out even.*
You know what he means, millions of homeless
wandering the country, displaced by dams, industrial
zones, the Olympics. "I wandered lost to many

villages until I came here and made up my mind

Stop. Here. My stay-put home.

I took for my own this empty house,

whose family left to work in Industrial Zone.

Many empty houses—you can have

any one you like." "I want you

to take me to U.S.A.,"

said Moy Moy. "A Chinese farmer—

nothing. A maker of the mouse in an electric brain

factory—nothing." The nightingale in the cage above

their heads sang along with the talking, and scattered

seeds and spattered water down upon the talkers

(and their food). A bare lightbulb hung next

to a wall, to be lit for emergencies and holidays.

In the dark, Moy Moy told

her failure: She's never married.

"During the Great Calamity, women acted

married to one husband, and another husband,

and another. I had no one. No one

but this brother waiting for me at the agreed-

upon place." Lai Lu told

his failure: "I have no children."

Wittman told his failures: Not

staying with his wife till death us do part.

His son not married. Never getting
a play on Broadway, New York. Not
learning enough Chinese language.
(Marilyn Chin says, "The poet must read
classical Chinese. And hear Say Yup.")
Midnight, Lai Lu stood, said,
"Ho, la. Good sleep, la."
He left for some back room. Moy Moy
said, "Follow me." Wittman followed her
out the front door. White stones
studded the courtyard walls;
a jewel-box up-poured stars into sky.
Followed the queue of black hair gleaming
in the black night, hied through alleys that turned,
and again turned, and again, 3 corners
in, and entered a home through an unlocked
door. "No one lives here.
You may live here." She parted curtains.
The bed was a shelf, like a sleeper on Amtrak.
She backed into the cupboard, scooted, and sat.
Her pretty bare feet swung. He
sat beside her. "Heart Man, marry me."
He ought to kiss her. But they don't have
that custom, do they? He was a virgin for Mongolian

women. Aged, married too long,

the body refused to spring and pounce and feast,

to make the decision for sex. He reached for and held

her hands. "Moy Moy." Oh, no,

shouldn't've said her name. Can't fuck

Younger Sister. "Thank you for wanting me

to marry you." Her hands felt trusty. "Marry"

said, and "marry" heard many times tonight.

Taña appears. She's sitting on the other side of him;

that's her, warm pressing against him. He

could see her in the dark, her whitegold

hair, her expression; she's interested, curious,

pissed off. He tapped her bare foot

with his bare foot. She's solid.

A red string ties her ankle to

his ankle. No string connecting him and

the other woman. He spoke to the not-hallucinated

one. "You're the most beautiful Chinese

woman I've ever met. I dearly want

to kissu, suck lips with you."

Say anything; Taña doesn't know

Chinese. "Thank you, you want to marry me."

A rule of the open road: Keep thanking.

"However, I don't want more marriage.

Our son, my one son doesn't have any marriage.
No one. Will you marry him?" Wittman
dismayed and amazed himself. Forever, then.
Forever husband. Forever father. Never
lust after a woman again but wish her
for his lonely son. I wish for Mario
a life's companion. "My son, Mario,
makes good money. He knows power
tools and car mechanics. He can cook.
He has some college. He is kind
and intelligent, and I want for him a kind
and intelligent person." The old Chinese
customs aren't so bad; fix him up
with a wife, a daughter-in-law of my own choosing.
Moy Moy's holding of his hand became
a handshake. "Dui dui dui,"
she cooed. "We will agree on a place to meet.
He will be waiting for me there. Ho, la.
Good night, la. Good sleep, la-a-a."
(You do not need vocabulary to understand
the Chinese. Just feel the emotion
in *la-a-a* and *ahh* and *mo* and *aiya*.)
Moy Moy left. Taña, also, left.
I am alone in the dark, so dark that

nothing exists but my thoughts, and thoughts
are nothing. Came all the way to China,
and failed to fuck another besides my long-
wedded spouse before I die.

                           The next thing,
dust was falling like ash, like glitter. Far
away, so faint, maybe imaginary, crowed
a rooster. Another, closer, rooster answered,
took up the opera, and another, and another,
each rooster louder, the loudest blaring
right outside the window. Wake up
in a village in China. Go use the community

toilet. Wash up in the town square,
brush teeth, swab down with the guys.
The women clean themselves indoors.
"Ho sun." "Ho sun." "Ho sun."
"Ho sun." Good morning. Good
body. Good belief. Good letter.
A happy civilization, glad to see
one and all, every morning. "Help me
farm rice?" asked Brother Lai Lu.
He took Wittman's hand. 2 men
are walking China hand in hand. They walked
to the field for planting on this hopeful day.

They wrapped seedlings in cloth, settled the bundles
in baskets, tied baskets to waist, and waded
into the paddy. Oooh, the mud, the pleasureful
mud, my free and happy toes. You trace
in water a square, and at each corner embed
one rice plant. Oh, my hands
rooting and squishing silken luscious mud.
Look up: A line of rising and bending
people—kids too—are coming toward
our line. (The kids are all boys.
The girls have been adopted out to the most loving,
well-educated parents in the West. Chinese
girls will take over and improve America.)
Children, everybody growing mai.
Plant toward someone who's planting toward you,
and make straight rows. Perfectly quiet,
we're sighting and pacing one another, and organizing
the water into small and large rectangles, stitching
a silvery quilt over Mother Earth.
Every jade-green spikelet has its jade-
green water double. 2 infinite
blue skies. Slow white clouds
form, move and change, and wisp away.
Me, the one amid all of it taking

note. In the silence, critters peeping,
buzzing, chirping, humming, seem to be
my own mind idling and making it up—
but a frog jumps, a dragonfly zooms.
Tadpoles—schools of tadpoles—hurry by.
A mudsnail gliding and sliding. And me
planting rice, helping to feed a fifth
of the world's people. All, all related.
This planting food together is heart
center. Hour after hour, eon after eon,
doing the same thing, plant, plant,
sink, loft, into water, into sky,
I am one of the human race that has always
done this work. Stay, let this life be
my whole life, and these people my people.
That other life, the one in America, the wife,
the son, the Berkeley education, that
complex life is dream. Stay
and see the rice through to harvest. How
long does it take for rice to grow through
its seasons? A year? Two years? Now
that I've found this lost possible self—Chinese
rice farmer—let me stay with it. Keep
doing this most basic human task

til satisfaction. When used to this life
and don't *see* it anymore, then leave.

BAD VILLAGE

                    Once more, away,
out on the open road, Wittman enjoyed
his walk with fellow travelers. Millions errant,
looking for work, some on paid vacation.
The driver of a pony cart slept atop
his produce; his pony knew the way. A buffalo
or ox pulled a tumbrel of logs and rocks;
woodcutter and wife dozed side by side.
A bicyclist carried one bar of steel
under an arm. Another bicyclist was delivering
a circus of chairs. Motorbikers covered
faces, and entire heads, with gauzy scarves,
no helmet law. 100
big white ducks or geese rode
on the roof of a bus, feathers ruffling; they
did not try to fly away. A stake
truck and a flatbed truck, both
honking hard, drove head-on

at each other, veered to drivers' right,
and passed. They're right-laners, like us.
People walking carried twigs, furniture,
baskets, pots, live fish in buckets.
Wittman changed his walk to be like other
Peripatetics. Cut out the American
attitude. Quit the truckin', the I'm-walkin'-here.
Send the strength away from macho shoulders,
and will it down to butt seat chakra.
Walk bent-legged, loose-kneed,
loose-seated like kung fu.
Hands behind relaxed back. Oh,
it feels so good, giving in—bent old
China Man at long last. A pickup
truck bounced, braked—off popped
a giant pig, a hog. PLOP! Burst?!?
But it got to its feet, jiggled, breathed loud,
coughed, coughed, and screaming, ran off.
Some men in the laughing crowd gave
chase, Wittman too. They were running
after a big fat naked person.
Her pink Caucasian ass and hams rolled
and pumped. Hurrying ahead of the hooting, joking
crowd, she screamed, grunted, wheezed. Internal

injuries. Ran toward people who were assembling
a market. Help me. Help me. Please. She
was It, the big fat naked dumb one. Caught.
The redoubling crowd herded the sow back
to the truck. She climbed the ramp. Her owner kicked
her legs out from under her, thanked the people,
and drove off. No pig basket for
her. So what if she's hurt? On her way
to slaughter anyway. Wittman reentered
the village that the sow had led him to. Today
was market day; farmers were arriving with this day's
harvest. Cooks were boiling up noodles
for breakfast, throwing in handfuls of meat and choy.
There was an empty stool in a hovel restaurant;
he sat down amid the slupping, slurping men,
and let himself be served what everybody else
was having. (You're charged extra for the seat; sitting
is a luxury.) (No ladies. Ladies cook
and eat at home.) The men sat close,
knee to knee, thigh to thigh, but not
quite touching. Did bump elbows.
They ate fast. 2 fingers tap-
tapped the table—another luxury, a table—
got refills. Tap tap. Thanks

thanks. The cook himself came around
with the tea. Some people lift-lifted it
toward the others. Sociable Wittman lift-
lifted, nod-nodded to one and all.
Tap tap. Thanks thanks. Abruptly,
eaters pushed away from the table, paid,
and left. Lazy guys stayed on,
lit cigarettes, talked. One man
folded himself up on his stool, arms
wrapped around knees, and slept. Chinese
can sleep anywhere. Our American
did not understand any of the speaking,
he'd traveled that far. Can't stand to be
left out. Act as though you get it.
They spoke a spit dialect, like Daffy Duck
and Sylvester the Cat. And they held long notes,
ho-o-o, who-o-o-o. Laugh when they laugh.
They didn't seem to be talking about him; they
weren't referring to him with their squinty sly
eyes. The spitter with yellow tobacco fangs,
Sylvester, looked straight at him, and asked
something. Yes, nodded the agreeable American.
Yes. Sylvester and Daffy glanced at each other.
Complicity. Good, they seemed to say, let's

go, let's do it. They stood, paid,
waited for Wittman to pay, saw his wallet,
watched him pay with a bill that made
the proprietor use up all his change.
He walked deliberately step by step up to
the suspected muggers, and said in English, "Don't
you mess with me, bro. You're gonna get what for.
You're gonna get what's comin' to ya.
You mess with me, you messin'
with the Man." He reached inside his shirt
for his gat. The bravos vamoosed. Onlookers,
who will gather at any commotion, gave way.
And spread the word: armed man, American
with a gun, come to town. Whichever twisty
turning meandering path he took, Wittman
felt people keeping slant eyes on him.
And so, as the bad stranger, he arrived at
the meat market. The halves of a boiled hairless
dog hung by meat hooks through
its eye sockets. Paws in begging posture.
German shepherd? Labrador retriever?
Parents have brought children to watch the butcher
do something to it with a knife. At another
stall, a tub of piglets, like human babies,

some dead, some but stunned, alive
and moving, bloodied. A customer chose a snake
from jars of live snakes, haggling price
all the while. The snake man squeezed
the sides of its head, the jaws opened,
the fangs shot milk, which he caught in a bowl.
Just when you're feeling relief, they aren't harming
those snakes, he killed one, drove
a nail through its head. (So this
is the ancient culture that Chinatown defends
against the Department of Public Health and PETA?)
Wittman stayed in that town. Don't turn away.

Face what's real. Fix my reputation.
He found a hotel, a house with door wide
open, showing a front room with cots as
furniture. The crony witch widow woman
pointed at each bed, choose, choose,
you choose, first guest, no
other guest. Ah, but there's more;
she led him to a ladder, indicated up
up, you up. The loft was the private
one-bed room, fit for a rich tourist.
He paid her, held out money, let her take
however much the charge. Then up ladder

again, and fell into the rag nest bed.
Sick. Gave in to illness, every
part of his body ill. Ceiling and walls
waved, buckling, fluttering. He'll tilt
and roll off the edge of the loft into
darkest China. Hot. The roof? Fever?
Time spirals in China. In America, it shoots
straight out, like the line on the heart monitor
of the dead. The line faded between forever
and instance, awake and asleep, actual and dream.
It seems, at some twilight, the widowlady
witch fed him a brew, a medicine or a poison.
So kind or wicked of her, too old
to be climbing ladders, yet climbing the ladder
to take care of him. The ladder was missing.
No escape. He had memory of it: one pole
taller than the other, for climbing up to the mesa-
like rooftop, and down into the kiva,
when I was an Indian, a San Ildefonso
Indian, former life. I'll make the witch
happy, recognize her, she and I were
girlfriend and boyfriend. I know
she recognizes me too, ministering to me so
nicely, palming my brow. I hear voices.

I can understand them; they're plotting to steal
my money. All she had to do was ask.
I fanned out my money, take, take.
But she wants my life. Do I have a soul?
I can't feel my soul. I think soul
is something we have to imagine. Want
soul, imagine one. Like imagining I have
it in me to be a husband, a father. Imagine
the peaceful dark, and you go into the peaceful
dark. Imagine the white light, and you enter
and become the white light.

       May all beings be safe from danger.

       May all beings be safe from danger.

       May all beings be safe from danger.

       May all beings be safe from danger.

A gold ribbon arises and flies and winds
around the woman on the ground floor and around
the man in the loft, and shines through walls
and curls and twirls around every neighbor
and neighbor's neighbor and the big pig
and her baby pigs and the dogs and snakes and geese
waddling the earth and geese flying in air, and
spans oceans all the while looping
dolphins and whales and sharks and small fish

and the flying fish spangling and leaping like the ribbon
itself lacing and embracing each and every
living thing all the way to the other
hemisphere to hug my own true love
and our own dear child and all people
our own people and returning to include me.
Aloha kākou. May there be love
among us, love including me.
Oh, I am loved. I am loved.

With such good feelings, the pilgrim recovered
from illness-at-the-world and illness-at-China.
The pig chasers, the would-be thieves, the dog and
snake butchers, the witchy innkeeper
took their places as ordinary people, as ordinary
as himself. Wittman got up, well, and traveled on.

Now, I, Maxine, could let Wittman die,
let him die in the China of his dreams,
and proceed on this journey alone. He's lived
a full life, life enough, China
enough. Loved wife and child; they
loved him back. Planted rice. Read
some good books. Felt happiness, felt

gratitude. Enough. But I don't like
traveling by myself. I ought to learn to go
places on my own, good for my character,
to be self-reliant. (A translation of my name,
Ting Ting, Self-Reliance. I should
live up to my name, Self-Reliant Hong.)
Why I need a companion, Monkey, along:
He's unafraid and unembarrassed to butt
and nose into other people's business.
He likes chatting with them and partying with them.
(I would rather hide, and spy, and overhear,
find out who people are when I'm not there.

Responsibly, sociably among them, I'm wont
to correct them, teach them, tell them Be happier.)
And he's able to enter the many places
in this world that a man is allowed and a lady
is not. And Wittman, a fiction, is free to befriend
anyone, and tell on them; he has no relatives
to be held hostage. I don't want to leave him dying,
sick and poor, destitute of health and money.
No airline ticket home. Passport
and identity stolen. The life of lowest poverty
is a meditation practice, a discipline, another
tale. Let me take him to one more

village, give him the commune of our bohemian
dreams.

ART VILLAGE

      Ming Ming. Bright Bright.
Double bright. He arrives at Ming Ming
in a rainstorm. Wind is driving the bamboo
and ginger and cane flat. No moment
between lightning and thunder. A logo
flashes. Ming Ming. A word we know,
sun and moon together, *bright*. 2
suns. 2 moons. Bright Bright.
Following the way the sign points, the wet
traveller runs to a village mired in mud,
into a courtyard that's a sty of mud. Ming Ming
seems to be a ghost town, yet
another ghost town whose denizens left
for a global city somewhere. He bursts in
to find an art studio, and artists painting
indoors during rain. They shout and laugh
like Welcome! Look at what the mew dragged in!
Like Get the man dry clothes and hot tea!

The nude model throws on her robe, and dashes
away to do their bidding. The men set
down brushes and palettes. Take 5.
They pull up stools and crates around the stove.
Wittman takes off his clothes, soaked
to the skin, and dons the robe the model brings
along with tea and wood and coal. "Thank you.
Thank you," the guest says in English,
his natural language, the best for giving
heartfelt thanks. "You well come,"
says a goateed artist. No, not
goatee. Let's give him a soul patch.
"Well, well," says a fellow with a ponytail.

"Koo. Koo. Koo." Cool. Cool.
They speak their English, which makes them laugh.
"How are you?" "I am fine.
Thank you." "You well come."
"I come from Heilongjiang. And you?"
Black Dragon River. The artists, communal
around the fire, brothers, smoking Peace
brand cigarettes and being served tea
and pastries, delight in trying out the Brave
language, the lingua franca taught in schools.
The cats are hip and up-to-date.
They wear their colors on worn, torn denim.

Some long hair. Some skinhead.

Black beards. Purple beard. 5

o'clock shadow, designer stubble. The old man

bewhiskered like that handsome Commie, Ho Chi Minh,

is home among his own kind. The artists

get to the extent of their English. Pots and buckets

plink and plunk; the roof drums. The paintings

are hung and stacked on the dry sides of the room.

Mr. Soul Patch brings to his lips

a xun, around which his hands fit perfectly,

and blows a music, old from long, long

ago. Our first male ancestor,

Bao Xin Gong, made the xun

of earth, made it earth-shaped, and gave

forth this sound that is the sound of time, from

far off to now to far after, the sound

of the animate winds, the yin wind and the yang

wind, the sound of the first man and this man

breathing song. Hear it, and it belongs

to you, and you belong to all of it.

The music ends on a long long

outbreath. The musician coughs and coughs,

spits a lunger onto the dirt floor,

rubs it in with his foot. Lights up

a cigarette. Urges the guest, Go on, go,
try it, blow. Wittman holds the earth xun
in spread hands, fingertips over some
holes, brings it up to his mouth. Pásame
la botella. The sound he gives out
is low, definite, smooth, clear, loud.
"Koo." "Koo." "Tell me about xun."
The artists—they are masters of many arts
in this commune of makers—speak with numbers.
7,000. Xun was unearthed? invented?
7,000 years ago? In the year
7,000? 40. The xun in your hand

is 40-something—generations? years?
Cough cough. Pat-patting the lungs,
the heart, me, myself. 40. The musician
who takes up the xun will die in his 40s.
All artists die young. We sacrifice.
The painters, the model too, have coughs. The smoke,
inhale, cough, exhale, cough, cough.
The elder artist can't help lecturing
the younguns about their health. "No wonder
you Chinese chronically cough and spit.
You, with every breath, you're drawing microbes,
germs, disease from that old, used instrument,

into your respiratory system. Those xun
players died young because they caught an illness
from this infected instrument, which they passed on to you.
You guys shouldn't be living in your studio."
Points at the beds, the stove, the tables loaded
with cans, bottles, tubes of chemicals, food.
"You're handling poisons all day,
and breathing fumes all night. I know.
My wife's an artist. We've been poor,
but she keeps her workplace, her art lab,
away from where we eat and sleep. She wears
a face mask, a respirator. Just like
Chinese do in traffic. And, come on,
don't smoke. Don't smoke. If you
knew your history, you wouldn't smoke.
Only 3 grandmothers ago,
BAT, British American Tobacco,
forced our people to buy opium, and tobacco-
opium mix. We had two wars
Chinese versus Anglos,
Opium War I and Opium War II.
We lost both times. We fought back
poison against poison, and guns, sold
bread with arsenic at the bakeries for Westerners.

When I learned my history, I stopped smoking
cigarettes, pot, any kind of shit."
The young artists don't understand
a thing he says, else they'd laugh over
the bakerman, bakerwoman guerrillas.
They do know, they give their lives for xun,
for art. They take his waving and pointing to mean
admiration for them and their work. They open
albums full of photos of paintings with prices.
Their brushwork takes your breath away.
The lines and angles of Picasso. The impasto
of Van Gogh. The colors of Rothko.

The icing of Thiebaud. They can do anything.
But where is the new, the never-before-seen
that we're counting on the post-Liberation
post–Cultural Revolution generation
to give us? Art schools in the U.S.
are folding their painting classes, teaching computer
and industrial design. The young artists show
the old artist (buyer? patron?) their portfolios.
Chinese kids selling their art
on the streets of Sydney, Florence, San Francisco.
On these walls, their latest work: dark
pictures. Heavy black crosses. Black

cross in foregrounds crossing out whatever else.
Black cross in backgrounds or upper
corners, a coming menace. The New China
still hung up on Christianity.
Let it go already. But look,
we're painting exactly what we see
before our very eyes. There, above
your head—the stovepipes, one up through
the roof, and 2 arms out the walls.
Like the number 10.   ✝   We are painting
hearth and home. The world will see Crucifix.
Chinese viewers will read personal
messages, and political messages. And the government
read forbidden messages, and the artists get
into trouble. And what is that above the door,
the kiva, hogan door? Eagle, you are here.
Bear, you are here. Bear, protector
of journeys west. Dragonfly, you
here too. And Snake. And Coyote, you,
here. And Zia, sun and sipapu.
Kokopelli on flute. Whirling Logs,
like Buddha's hairs, like swastikas.
All bordered by beansprouts, river
waves, whirlwind. And the threshold

lintelpiece itself border, land
bridge, rainbow. "Nicolai Fechin,"
say the artists. "Nicolai Ivanovich Fechin."
They name the woodcarver who made this icon,
and placed it at this threshold, that we be
aware coming in and going out that
we, people and animals, migrated across the top
of the world. They came our way; we
went their way. All connected with all,
all related. The rain stops. The painter
with the purple beard motions Come come,
and leads the way through the mud to his home
and studio. "Nicolai Ivanovich Fechin. . . ."
They stand before a wet oil. The paint
wet but also a river rushing, mud, and men,
men drowning? mouths wide open
crying Help? No, they are cheering and
laughing—Eureka! The pan is full of gold!
They—Chinese American Forty-Niners—
fall into the gold-giving water,
and roll in it. In joy. In fear. O,
Comrade of Californians! You we left
behind know and care what became of us
who went to Gold Mountain and never returned.

O, Artist. Draw *me*. *See* me.
Show me beautiful, old. "Draw *you*,"
says Purple Beard. Dui. Dui. Dui.
So, for long sessions of time, the wanderer
holds still as the artist draws and paints him.
The artist looks and looks, squinting his eyes,
to see everything, what's there, the visible,
and what's not visible, only he can see.
Suddenly, at a break, at a meal, Purple Beard's
face comes up close to Wittman's
face. He's studying my profile.
Tonight by electric light, the left profile;
this morning the right profile, the 3
quarters profile, the angles the eyelids
open and shut, the ear, the other ear,
the hairline, the texture and many colors
of hair and skin, the lines, the creases. Eyes
asquinch, he's studying me, breathing, smelling me.
He hasn't begun the actual painting, won't
begin until he's made studies and decisions.
Here, let's work in the courtyard,
the light from the north. No, let's go
indoors, this house, the light
from the south. The artist faces the sitter,

looks and draws, draws and looks, and one
day decides: Fullface. Good.
The face I myself looked at every
morning first thing back in the life
where bathrooms had mirrors. Full on. I, the writer,
look in the mirror more than the normal person.
To know my mien. *Mien* same-same
Chinese, English. To track and trace
momently changes. That's me, still good-
looking. But can't hold any one
expression for long. Hold it, and you freeze up.
Think upon looks, and that vanity shows.

Try method acting. For lovingkindness
in the eyes, look upon the other lovingly,
kindly. Purple Beard works without
talk, can't understand him anyway,
makes you quiet down yourself, likewise
be without talk. Be Nobody. He's
making an idol of me, admiring, adoring me so.
Lately, Taña doesn't draw her husband,
doesn't use her art on him. Doesn't give him
her artist's interest, regard him, record him, behold
him, find beauty in him. She disdains "narration."
She paints lines and spaces like calligraphy

that's not words. She can't stand Frida Kahlo—
"Too much narrative. Too much pain."
All the way to China to get appreciation.
Taña would love it here, among this commune
of artists. No, no, she wouldn't. She
wouldn't live like these girls. Bicycling
away rain or shine to run an errand
for her artist. Coming back with cigarettes, food
supplies, art supplies, coal, wood,
money. They aren't so very communal;
each woman serves just her one
boyfriend. We're back to the days of
James Joyce and Henry Miller, women
living to serve genius. Taña would organize
a cultural revolution. Girls, *you*
can be the artists of your dreams. She'd
see to it that this village dine together.
Everyone cooks for all. Give dinner
parties, be civilized. You ALL come.
Walt Whitman: "I will not have a single
person slighted or left away." But Taña
and these artists same-same: Once they regard
a thing, it becomes treasure. Surprise:
I'm not bored sitting day after day.

I'm old, worked for a lifetime, time
to rest. Chinese know about working
hard, and give rest as a gift. "Sit.
Sit," they invite the guest. "Sit, la."
You take the crate or stool or the one chair
(Chinese invented chairs), saying,
"No, no, *you* sit, la,
don't stand on ceremony, thank you,
thank you." Purple Beard crouches, peers,
takes a kung fu step forward,
a tai chi step back, moves himself and
his metal easel right beside his subject,
paints, paints, backs away, easel
and all, paints some more. Turns his back
on the model and the picture, holds up a hand
mirror, and looks at their images in reverse,
turns around quick—catches something—
paints it down. As if I am
hard to see. The artist is doing mighty
feats of concentration to hold me real.
Across the courtyard is a south-facing
window, dark inside, nobody lives there.
One day, the window is utterly gone.
Nary a jamb or corner or glint remains.

The explanation has got to be that tree;
it leafed out, and put the window out
of sight. Must've mislooked, imagined
a window through the wavering spaces between
glittery leaves. Then, another day,
the leaves disappear, the tree disappears.
A green tree? A red tree? Gone.
And there's the window again. Next to the window
is a gray wall. There are no shadows
on it because no tree, no branches.
Only light, light that changes, changes
with the moving day. So beautiful, the non-
repeating universe, I could watch it forever.
So beautiful, the nothingness of the ground.
Suddenly, the artist picks up the painting,
turns it around, thrusts it toward its subject—
"Finis!"—and has him see his portrayal. Omigod!
So much strain. So many wrinkles.
Read the wrinkles. I'm straining might and main
to carry out ideals. I have ideals.
I didn't lose them along with my young self.
But I try too hard, the strain shows.
Not graceful under fire. I ended
the war in Viet Nam. I am determined,

we shall stop warring in Iraq,

and Afghanistan. Well, not

the fun-loving monkey but the world-carrying

citizen, okay. Wittman leaves

the art village, leaves the picture for history.

SPIRIT VILLAGE

He betakes himself to yet one more village.

I need him to go to an all-male place,

a monastery, to make sure that Shao Lin

or Han Shan or Water Margin sanctuary

exists. That the Chinese religion lives.

He locates and climbs Su Doc Mountain.

(Su Doc, Think Virtue, Hong

Ting Ting's father's name.) Through

the fog and mist of dragons breathing, following

a trail, possibly made by deer, he comes

to a ramshackle *mew,* a temple. No one

answers his knock. He opens the door, and enters

a dark room. Silent men and a few

little boys are eating supper. Someone

hands over a rice bowl and chopsticks,

and gestures eat eat. The food
is leftovers of leftovers. Even
the child monks practice eating meditation,
mindfully selecting some unrecognizable
brown vegetable, chewing it many times,
tasting it, identifying it, thinking about
and appreciating who grew it and cooked it, grateful
to them, and to the sun and the rain and the soil,
and all that generates and continues all.
After eating (food still left over),
the monks sit enjoying stomachs full,
holding the segue from this present moment
to this present moment. The kid monks
play kung fu boxing, push and
chase one another unreprimanded
around the table. The floor-sitting adults
get up. With sand and a small pail
of precious water, each cleans his bowl.
No leader tells the newcomer
what to do; no explainer gives
instructions. Under the vow of silence, we
can know we are all equally human.
Can't tell who's smarter than who,
whose job is better, who has more

money, more class. Silence, democracy.
Enemies can't argue; thoughts and feelings
deepen, alter, fade, merge. The monks go
outdoors and meander in the dusk
that shadows into dark night. You
can see the Milky Way, the River of Heaven,
bridge, trail of corn, diadem
made up of individual stars.
It's not a long wispy cloud as in light-
polluted America. *Dok dok dok.*
Dok dok dok dok dok.
The sound of wood clapping on wood calls

the community back inside. This monastery
is so poor, it doesn't own a bell.
They've transformed the room where they'd eaten
into a meditation hall. Candlelight
and incense and *dok-dok-dok* summon
deities. They arrive upon the altar.
There's Kwan Yin the merciful. And Kwan Yin
the wrathful. She who imprisoned Monkey, and freed
him. And red Gwan Goong on his red horse;
that book he's reading is *The Art of War.* The 8
Immortals are here too, and lohans and arhats
and Buddhas and monkeys. We offer this incense

to all Buddhas and bodhisattvas throughout
space and time. The cushion in the middle place
among the monks is empty, for the new brother.
The community is aware of his presence; they look
after him. I will stay and sit until—
satori! Where else but in China?
Breathe in . . . breathe out . . . breathe
in . . . breathe out . . . breath incoming . . .
breath outgoing . . . breath incoming . . .
These monks don't have a chanter guiding
their meditation. Peeking at them, you can't tell
who's meditating, who's acting.
Surely, nobody here's an actor, a spy
in government pay. Why would Commies bother
with a temple in the middle of nowhere?
No one hits Monkey upside the head
for mind-wandering. He tries signaling a need
for a whack, taps himself on a shoulder blade,
taps himself on the head. No minder monk
whacks him with a Zen stick. But *Zen* is Jap-
anese, and *satori* is Japanese. The monks
sit on, the kid monks gone,
to play, to do schoolwork, to sleep.
Monkey would quit too but for his sense

of competition and peer pressure.

The usual workings of his mind take him over;

he plays the time game: 29 . . .

30 . . . 40 minutes . . . 1 hour . . .

2 hours . . . 3 . . . real time?

Seeming time? It feels 9 o'clock,

then at length, or shortly, 11 o'clock.

How to be in sync? Whyfor in sync?

Because joy and life exist nowhere but the present.

Dok dok dok dok dok.

At last, the monks stir, wake up,

massage their feet, pound their own shoulders,

walk about, go out, come

back, unroll the cushions, which become beds,

blanket, and pillow. Meditation hall

becomes dorm. Wittman does get tap-

tapped, on the feet. A monk about to bed

down beside him tap-taps him, and makes

a circle motion with his hand: Turn around.

You dis the gods, giving them the underside

of your feet. And your head will benefit

exchanging vibes, chi, dreams with the altar.

Candles burn down. Shadows on the ceiling

fly into night. Snoring, snuffling,

vocalizing—*aaahh, oooo, rrrrr*—the community

sleeps together. Breath breathing breath.

Dok dok dok. Wake up.

4 a.m. Time to meditate again.

Everybody gets back up to sitting

position, and breathes out, breathes in,

aware of breathing out, aware of breathing in.

When I, Maxine, am worried and can't sleep,

I remember to remember: at 4 a.m.

the Dalai Lama and William Stafford are awake

with me, and meditating and making up

a poem, and making up the world, preparing

the morning that we can

live as peaceful gentle,

kind human beings. We build the Kaya,

the Body, and the Dharmakaya,

the Buddha-body. Hold our bluegreen

world joyous and vibrant. *Mm nn*

mm nn mm mmm . . . no no . . .

I am hearing Heart Sutra in Chinese.

Heart Sutra that won the war for the Vietnamese.

People awake around the globe turning and

lifting day into being chanting

Heart Sutra. No eye, no

ear, no nose, no tongue,

no body or mind, no form,

no sound, no smell, no taste,

no touch, no object of mind,

nor feelings, nor perceptions, nor

mental formations, nor consciousness.

All things are empty. Nothing

is born, nothing dies. No ill-

being, no cause of ill-being,

no end of ill-being. No

old age and death, no end

to old age and death. Wu wei.

Wu wei. Wu wei. Now,

not heart Sutra. Older than Heart.

Tao. Wu wei. Wu wei.

No way. No thought. No

doing. No willing. Dwell no-

where. Rest in nothing. How did no

bang the universe to life? No answer.

Dok dok. Dok dok dok.

Next, go outdoors to play / work /

fight / dance / move chi kung fu.

Begin, stand, root into earth,

root like tree. Knees bent, seat

heavy, feel chi, imagine chi
rise up through the soles of your feet.
Lift arms, pull the chi from the earth
up to the sky. Circle the Sky. Stir
the Universe. The police in Tiananmen Square
watch for lift-arms—first move
of Falun Gong. They're Falun Gong. Arrest them.
Commies haven't lost belief in the old ways,
that chi kung can turn heaven and earth.
Revolution. Forest moves, leaves and insects,
weather, dirt, and water blow and flow.
The kung fu movers enter and emerge
in and out of the camouflage of trees.
A person stands out, tall against
the sky, like a shining angel, then shrinks
into a human bug flickering in the landscape.
The martial artists make animal moves, get
animal powers. Cup hands downward,
like paws, up on hind legs—rabbit,
bear, monkey. Arms and legs fly—
white crane, invented by woman.
Make 108 moves
108 times, keep
existence going, cause life and the good

to come into being. The 360
meridians of the world stream with the 12
meridians of my body. I swirl,
galaxies swirl. Rocks alive, mountains
alive. Soul through and through rocks,
mountains, ranges and ranges of mountains.
Bright Smile of Spontaneous Joy. Lift
the sides of your obstinate mouth, and start joy.
Joy courses through the body, all
the happy bodies. "Come come come,"
beckons a monk. "Lai, la. Lai, la.
Come see a monk in ecstasy.

We have a monk in ecstasy."
The cell has no windows and no lights
but you can still see. A tall man
is standing tilted, curving to one side.
Round. His body seems to make a round.
Head back and uplifted. You can't
see if his eyes are open or shut. So,
this is the way it looks from the outside.
A perfection. The witnesses make silent applause,
alleluia hands, jubilation hands.
"Lai, la. Lai, la."
Now to the hillside with a willow stream

that's a graveyard. This stone like a door
marks the grave of Fa Mook Lan,
Woman Warrior. Over Wittman's shoulder,
I can read each word of her name.
"She killed herself," says the monk.
"She hung herself." No. No.
Why? I can't believe it. Why?
"The emperor heard: The mighty general was a woman
in disguise, a brave and beautiful woman who'd gone
to war as a man. He sent for her to be a wife.
She refused, and he placed her under house arrest.
She killed herself at home." No. No.
She can't be the Fa Mook Lan who's
the woman warrior I told about, we all
tell about. Many women named for her.
And the monk's speech, a rare dialect issuing
from the habit of silence, hard to understand.
She couldn't have killed herself. She couldn't
have found life after war, life
as a woman, useless to live. How to go on
without her? Wittman has to find a way.
And I have to find my own way.

VIET NAM VILLAGE

Go on, alone. I have no
sense of direction. Left, right, east,
west arbitrary to my instincts. Mother
taught me, Memorize: Face the black rocking
chair, place your arms on its arms;
the scissors, the pencil you hold in *this* hand
this side of the rocking chair. I've been
lost, taking a walk with our toddling son
into nature. Sun upon and between the shaking
leaves forms images of rivers and houses and people
coming to the rescue. I shouted and screamed for rescue.
Our boy said, "We can eat the flies."
I've been lost, taking a solitary walk
in my own neighborhood, where the streets curve
around, and I circle and circle. Earll drove
around until he found me. I walked very,
very mindfully into the Grand Canyon,
down the Great Unknown, lost sight
of any person, and did not get lost,
and walked back up to the top. I followed
a deer, who did not run away from me,

and I did not get lost. Maps of China
were made for me by Columbus and Kafka.
The most beautiful thing that Columbus had ever seen
was the land, "gardens," wholly bright green.
He walked among the trees, which grew 5 kinds
of leaves and fruit branching from one trunk.
The greatest wonder in the new world, he said, was
"diversity." A man alone in a canoe paddled by;
he was bringing bread from island to island.
Kafka heard from an unknown boatman
that a great wall will be built to box in
the Center, which is itself a series of box mazes,
all contained within the endless outside
wall. Villages, cities, each further maze.
The ruler of the Center has a message for us;
he whispers it into the messenger's ear, has it
whispered back, nods, then dies.
To get to us, the way goes from innermost
courts, up mountains of staircases
and stiles over walls, down stairs
and more stairs to an outer palace, onward
to the next outer palace, the next, more
courts, more stairs, more mazy
palaces. Years and years go by.

And I am traveling the other way, inward
to the Center. Must not tire, must
not grow old and want to die.
After years and miles of travel and worry,
keeping west, keeping south, I come
to a home-like village in Viet Nam.
All the land from the Yangtze River
to Quang Tri had been Nam Viet / Nan Yue.
The Hung / Hong Bang kings ruled
for 2,621 years.
I was on a boat in the Pearl River delta
(my mother in a boat going the other way,
hiding under a pile of oranges, escaping
from the Japanese, catching the big ship
to meet my father in America), and next
thing I knew, I was in the Red River delta.
The same pearlescent water, changing colors
with the tropical sun, the same red dirt,
and gray dirt and black dirt. Same
as the San Joaquin delta, back home. The farmers
grow rice; they treasure the water
buffalos, name them names like Great Joy.
The people look same-same Chinese.
"The like of the same I feel,

the like of the same in others. . . ."
But an utterly foreign language chimes out
of their mouths. (Flashback to the first day of
American school: Other children! But
I can't speak with them. I wanted to say,
"You smell like milk. Your skin
looks like chocolate ice cream. And yours
like strawberry-and-vanilla ice cream."
And I wanted to ask, "How do you
feel being you?") I arrived
at the hamlet on a holiday. The hot
breeze, hot even beside the hurrying
river, blew and flew flags, long
banners, tassels, long ribbons. Lots
of red. Not just political red. Red
for health, for beauty, for good luck. *Clang*
clang clang clang! Bang! Bang!
Ho-o-nk! Qwoooo! Bum! Bum! The musicians
played freestyle no-pattern
free-for-all any old way. Broke
patterns. Broke time. And firecrackers
went off every which way.
Firecrackers like bombs and artillery fire,
and rocket fire. They aren't afraid,

the bangs setting off P.T.S.D.
No more P.T.S.D. P.T.S.D. over.
War over. War won. They won every war.
The American War, and before that, war
with the French, and before that, the Japanese,
and before that, the Chinese. They
invited me into a tent open
on one side, sat me at the picnic
table, and served me joong. Just like
back home. Untie the string—what
message are these lines and knots telling me
if I could but read? Unwrap the ti

leaves—ti sacred in every country
where it grows. Eat the rice and mung beans,
the pork, and the whole sun of egg yolk.
I partake of joong with the once-enemy.
Does joong mean to them what it means to me?
They are eating peace food with their
twice-enemy, an American, a Chinese.
Chinese invented joong to feed
the dragons in the river where Chu Ping, the peace
martyr, drowned himself. *Clang clang!*
Kang! Boom boom boom! Kang!
Bum bum! Kang kang! Qwoooo!

C'mon c'mon c'mon! I was rushed
out of the tent into a rushing crowd.
Everyone—all of the hamlet, and other hamlets—
out of the rolling ocean the crowd—around
corners and bends stream more crowd—
hurrying, hurrying somewhere wonderful. Above
heads, lifted and carried on chairs,
thrones, moved a parade of idols. Who
were they? Gods? Heroes? Ancestors?
They had big wide-open eyes, as if
they could see all things and all
people, see far to where we're going.
I could not recognize the idols by a sign,
no antler bumps on head, no
red face, no blue face,
no long ears, no mudra
of hands, no multiple hands, no
multiple heads. They looked like regular
people dressed up in silk and gold
raiment, and crowns. The crowd slowed, so
tight were we. We fitted ourselves breast to
back, sides to sides, no elbow poking, no
stepping on toes or heels. Over our heads,
the roomy sky was benign blue; the clouds

were long and wispy. The crowd up ahead
moved faster, drawing, pulling my part
of crowd after them, faster, faster. I'm
a short person. All I can see are backs.
Where are the friends I had joong with? I can't see
the idols anymore either. I look
at the sky trying but unable to project my point
of view to see the whole crowd, and the country it's
moving through, whether there's a destination,
and to find the people I know. I could lift
my feet, leave the ground, and the close-fitting
crowd would carry me. I don't have to watch

or decide where I'm going. I stayed in step,
running on tiptoes. The ground was dirt
and trodden grass. The dirt was damp, damper,
wet. We were beside the river. We were
following the snaking path of the long river.
Song Hong, River Red, the Red River,
which goes from the Yunan River in China
to the Gulf of Tonkin. The river is full
of dragons, the river *is* a dragon.
Viet Nam is a dragon rampant;
she has a large head, many mouths,
and a long spine that flares into fantails.

And *I'm* a dragon, and my mother a dragon. I
and all these people are drops of dragon within
the big dragon body. We are blood.
We are performing dragon. Every so often,
Chinese have to mass together,
become a mashing moshing crowd. In
the United States, lonely, you can join the people
in Chinatown shopping for their daily greens,
and get your fix of Chinese crowd.
But those crowds move in both directions,
pass one another coming and going.
This mass I'm embedded in
feels like a Japanese or Korean demo,
like an advancing army. Breaching worry (worry is
the default working of my natural mind), I feel:
elation. Crowd joy. Happiness-in-people.
I am reliving peace demonstrations.
In San Francisco, we were a peace dragon
with 100,000 pairs of feet
walking up and down the city hills. From rooftops
and balconies rained rice as at weddings,
and water on the summer's day, and rose petals,
and red and motley confetti. In Washington, D.C.,
on International Women's Day, 2003, our peace

dragoness was a mile long, winding our way
to the White House. 1,000,000 people
marched in Rome. And thousands of Shiite
and Sunni Muslims together in Baghdad.
"O Democracy, I will make inseparable
cities with their arms about each other's necks."
For the first time in history, the area in front
of the White House fence was banned to demonstrators.
The U.S. Park Police stopped us
at Pennsylvania Avenue. So, we sat in.
We sat ourselves down upon the historic
ground. "Our House, our street."

The Rangers are friendly and will converse, used
to being helpful to tourists. We have a permit;
didn't you get a copy? You promised,
we could parade in front of the White House.
"Our House, our street." The permit's
for only 25 people. Okay,
so let's count off 25.

1   2   3   4   5   · · ·

I was ninth, 9 my lucky number.
I said my number and stepped between the Rangers.
Running at us, whooping, cheering came
a pink-clad crowd—the tail of the dragon!

They had gotten through the police line
at the other end of Pennsylvania Avenue.
We rushed to meet them. Hugging, holding
one another, happy, we completed the ring
around our House. ". . . A troop gathers around me.
Some walk by my side and some behind, and some
embrace my arms or neck . . . thicker they come,
a great crowd, and I in the middle."
The encirclement lasted for moments, then the crowd
cooperated with the police, who asked them
and ordered them off the street. They retreated
to the borders of Lafayette Park. There they
stayed, keeping an eye on the 25 of us

who stood at the curb of the White House sidewalk.
In the middle of the park, drummers—Native Americans—
drummed banging day and night; the President
won't sleep til he calls off Shock and Awe.
Wave to the drummers, dance to the drumming. Sing,
and dance to our own singing, ululation,
and "Give peace a chance . . ." Wave
to the peace marchers, wave to the police, wave
to the children of Iraq. Everyone I saw was nonviolent.
The man with the bullhorn and the blowups of abortions
disappeared. Counterdemonstrators disappeared.

Slowly, imperceptibly moving so as not to provoke
violent arrest. Singing, "Salaam, peace,
shalom." We reached the White House fence.
Two grandmothers ago, our ancestresses
chained themselve to this black iron fence.
I held its bars in my hands, laid my face
against the barricade, and felt tears rise.
The other women were crying too, and cheering,
and dancing. Now the police saw, we had
unambiguously broken a law. Time
to start the arrests. All the police came
to attention, the Rangers blocking the left side

of the steet, the TAC squad the right, and the city
cops in a blue line facing us, the width
of the street between. On the White House
roof, a man in uniform aimed a high-
powered long-range sharpshooter
rifle at us. He aimed it, put it down,
aimed, put it down. A van drove
into the cordoned area; I think the insignia
on it said Federal Prison. 2 or 3
cops unfolded a tarp, and taped it on to
the side of the van, covering over the words.
I got afraid. They're hiding the place where

they would take us. They would disappear us.
They're going to drive us through the streets
of the capital in an unmarked white vehicle.
No one would know what became of us. Keep
singing. Keep loving. Say in unequivocal
words, "I love you." Hear, "I love you, Maxine."
The Metropolitan Police, the men, stood
in one-line formation. The women, we,
the demonstrators, drew one another close.
We were a bouquet knot of pink roses.
How can it be that all the cops are men,
and all for Peace women? I can't live
in such a world. I don't want to keep
living out the myth that men fight
and women mother. We regressed—the junior
high dance. One boy crossed
the wide floor, chose one girl,
escorted her back to the other side, where
he arrested her. "My wife
is gonna kill me," said a black cop;
"I'm arresting Alice Walker." "Don't hold
hands with me," said a white cop,
shaking off his partner, who was smiling up
at him; "Don't take my arm either."

They had each one of us stand by herself
alongside the van, and took our pictures.
"Quit smiling. What are you smiling for?
This is an arrest." This is your mug shot,
not your prom photo. I was smiling from
happiness; my government will not disappear me;
the tarp was but backdrop for shooting pix!
And the beautiful pink aura was still upon me.
My cop and I did not speak. A woman
officer in casual uniform, no gun,
took my purse, hair clips, pink poncho,
my earrings, and put them in a plastic bag.

Ready for handcuffing, I presented
my hands, wrists together, in front,
but my arresting officer signaled: in back.
I won't be able to write, to touch, to catch
myself, and will fall on my face. I turned about,
held my arms behind me as high as I could,
bending way forward, making my gestures
large for the witnesses to see. Handcuffs
in this age of new plastics work like the ties
for bread and trees. My arrester could
have tightened the cable-tie so that it cut
into the skin. The hands turn blue, burst.

These police were kind to tie us loosely.
Our belongings taken, our pictures taken,
handcuffed, we were made to get into
a paddy wagon, about 8 per wagon.
There are cages, like dog cages, between
the front seat and the side benches. I sat
in the middle of a bench, my shoulders touching
women's shoulders beside me, my legs touching
women's legs before me. Women outside
pounded, drummed on the van. Through the windshield,
we could see them applauding us. Somebody said,
"There's my daughter." The van started up;
the crowd parted, let the van through.
It got quiet. We were driving away from
the magic. The rose light went out.

I had nothing apposite to say, but
had to talk. "Now I'm on the trip
my father went on. In a paddy wagon to jail.
I'm reliving his arrests. I'm knowing his feelings.
Scared. Helpless. He wondered what would become
of him, maybe deportation. They're driving
him to the border, never to see his family again.
Oh, but my father wasn't committing civil

disobedience like us. He committed crime,
ran gambling, half the take in the city.
It was his job—go to jail, regularly.
Once a month, they raided the gambling house,
and took just one guy, my father.
He was all alone in the paddy wagon
riding through the streets and out of town.
It was okay. By the end of the night, he
was home. They let him go. He gave them money
and whiskey and cigarettes, and they let him go.
He gave them a fake Chinese name,
a different Chinese name every time;

he doesn't have a record." BaBa
used to say, "I want the life
you live." Now I'm living
the life he lived.
              A few women squirmed
out of their handcuffs, marveled at how
loosely they'd been tied. Arriving at the prison—
an immense spread-out building on bare land
fenced off from other bare land
in the middle of nowhere—they put their hand-
cuffs back on. We were taken to an office,
which had a wall that was a bank of jail cells.

We were separated, I in a cell by myself.
It was like a toilet stall; an unlidded
toilet faced the door. Also for sitting
was a little bench. Being little, I could
sleep curled up on it, just right.
At last, the solitary confinement of my dreams.
Nothing to fear. I could live here.
I could live here a long time,
and be content. As a girl, I knew
I could take solitary, if only I got
to see movies. Older, all I need
would be books and pencil and paper. But here I am,
and I don't feel like reading. And I don't
feel like writing. Can't write, hands
tied in back. Rest. Perfect rest.
And no more contending against shyness.
No more "sounded and resounded words,
chattering words, echoes, dead words . . ."
—Walt Whitman, lover of everyone and everyplace.
Yes, I could live like a cloistered nun,
but not have to pray for the good of the world.
Too soon, the jail door opened.
The cop whose wife is gonna kill him held
it open for Alice Walker. Now there's

a pair of us. I gave her my seat
on the bench, sat on the floor. She sat
various positions, cross-legged, almost
lotus, sat hunkered, arms hugging knees.
I'm glad, we've both had Buddhist practice, and know:
sit, be quiet. Breathe out.
Breathe in. I spoke, asked her
to undo my handcuffs, and if they
won't untie, to help me unbutton and lower
my pants, I had to pee. She got them off.
Kwan Yin, 2 more of your
10,000 hands, ma'am, reporting for duty,
for mercy. Being locked up with Alice,
I saw her: now a girl perched on a wall,
now we're under the dark moon and she's
shaman crone, now the sociable lady
on her book covers. She moves about in time.
Her time and ages circle through her. Now
her clothes flowed loosely on her thin body,
draped the edges of the bench; now roundly,
plumply she filled her blouse and long sweater.
I must look like that too; being small,
I could be a child still growing, or
I could be a shrinking old woman.

The light changes, the skin wrinkles, the skin
smooths.

The door opened again, we're a crowd
again, loud-speaking, loud-singing women.
"This little light of mine, I'm gonna let it shine.
Oh, this little light of mine, I'm gonna let it shine.
This little light of mine, I'm gonna let it shine.
Let it shine, let it shine, let it shine."
The singing connected the women in all this block
of cells; love and peace roused again.
"On the children of Iraq, I'm gonna let it shine.
Oh, on the children of Iraq, I'm gonna let it shine.
On the children of Iraq, I'm gonna let it shine.
Let it shine, let it shine, let it shine."
A nice woman cop came in, and asked us,
please to sing quieter, explained that they
couldn't hear to process us. We quieted,
pianissimo, "this little light of mine."
But impossible to keep it down. Crescendo. Waves.
"Let it shine, let it shine, let it shine."
Fortissimo. The door opened; a policeman
called a name, and took a woman away,
for booking. When my turn came, I couldn't

find my I.D. "The big cell for *you*
tonight." Tonight, overnight, I will
be with criminals, not sisters trained
in nonviolence. I asked the cop across
the desk from me—one prisoner and one cop
per desk; a woman was shackled to her chair
with old-style steel handcuffs,
couldn't be locked up because of illness—
I asked my arresting officer, please to bring
my bag of possessions, and let's go through it
again carefully for my I.D. Slowly,
he examined each thing. I talked-
story, "D'you know what I'm working on now?
I'm writing a Book of Peace. Once
in old China, there were books—reveries—
about how to end war. Those books were burned,
their authors' tongues cut out. My dream
is to write such a book for our time.
People who read it, I hope, will vow
not to use guns, not to use cluster bombs,
not any of the new weapons, plasma bomb,
neutron bomb, earth-penetrating bomb.
D'you mind letting me rummage
through my purse myself? Thank you. Thank you.

I seem to remember a secret compartment somewhere.
It's a trick purse. I brought it—pink,
sequins—especially for this demonstration.
And now it's fooling me. The hiding place
has disappeared. Let me try again.
Okay, it's not on this side. Let's try
upside down, backwards, unzip—
voilà!—here it is! My I.D.!"
And so I was charged with STATIONARY DEMO
IN A RESTRICTED ZONE—WHITE HOUSE SIDEWALK,
and let go. To appear in court for trial,
or else: A warrant will be issued for me, a wanted
felon, throughout the United States. The 24
women (25 counting a girl caught
up in the fun; her mother took her away,
bawled out everybody), the freed women
waited for one another, made sure
no one left behind. Where's the nearest
bus stop? No buses. Where's the subway?
"Far. You ladies don't want to
walk there. Dangerous." "Will you please
call us a taxi? 6 taxis?" "Cabs
won't come out here, ma'am. Please clear
the waiting area. Leave the waiting area

immediately." Then we were out on a road
in the middle of flat fields with nothing growing.
No stars in the sky, too lit
by the prison. Someone cell-phoned Code
Pink colleagues to come get us. The journalists—
journalists arrested too—turned on their equipment,
and recorded us exulting, the most beautiful day
of our lives. We rode back to the city
in cars festooned in pink ribbons, rode
showy through the capital of the U.S.A.
The good citizens cheered us, honked horns.
Not one disagreeing person

yelled or honked in anger. 12 days
later, Iraq War II, Operation Iraqi
Freedom, Shock and Awe started.

A-Day, hit Iraq with 300
to 400 satellite-guided missiles.
On the second day, round-the-clock bombing,
another 300 to 400
smart bombs. That was the plan, spoken by
an "author of Shock and Awe."
"You have this simultaneous
effect, rather like the nuclear weapons at Hiroshima,

not taking days or weeks but in minutes."
We had used all our arts—
sung, danced, walked about as goddesses.
Full body puppets on stilts, in pink
and red garments of flowing silk, bent
down in mercy to children. We staged
a theater of peace, recited poems—and did not
stop our country from war. I wanted to lie down
and die but did not. I do believe: Because
the world protested, the tonnage of bombs was not as
massive as planned. And we hit fewer civilians.
The peace we have made shall have consequences.
All affects all.

On parade in Viet Nam,
the dragon on hundreds of pairs of feet walked
and ran along the river—a river once red
with human blood from slaughter that these very
people around me eyewitnessed, and had part in.
We, dragon, ran and walked until
the village we'd left came into sight; the river
circled and returned us home. We rested in tents
and ate joong. I pointed, said, "Joong,"
hoping Chinese and Vietnamese
feed rice, beans, meat, 100-

year-old eggs wrapped in leaves
to the same ancestor, Peace, and to the dragons
who live in and *are* the river. But
they called this food something else,
and their story was about a beautiful princess
captured by / run off with a dragon.
All the village every year give
chase after her, and come home happy,
and in union.

FATHER'S VILLAGE

Follow the rivers and streams north,
deltas of Viet Nam turn into deltas
of China. There be my root villages.
23 years ago, from Guangzhou,
we had to hire a van and driver,
and a guide, get on 2 ferry boats—
drive, ferry, drive, ferry, drive
some more—the Pearl River's side
rivers winding and hairpin turning
at islands and bars. Had to stay overnight
in the one hotel, farmgirl maids

yell-talking, loud laughing, no sleep.
Drive on the next morning, and arrive
at Roots Headquarters for Long Lost
Overseas Relatives Finding Relatives.
Word, my father's name, my name,
had been bruited about this land. My cousin,
Elder Brother, heard, and was there to meet
me, recognized me, and greeted me, "Hola,
Younger Sister, our family is running in harmony."
"Hola, Elder Brother, our family is running
in harmony." *Harmony*. China has announced *Harmony*
its official theme. *Harmony* posted on walls.
Lights flash *Harmony* up on buildings;
the night rivers reflect *Harmony*. Our son,
a musician, has tattooed on each arm:

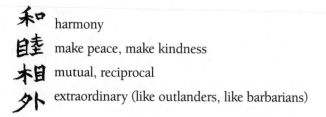

和 harmony
睦 make peace, make kindness
相 mutual, reciprocal
外 extraordinary (like outlanders, like barbarians)

I did the calligraphy myself.
Harmony also translates as *peace*;

its roots are *mouth* and *growing grain*. The mouth
speaks peace. Peace is food; peace nourishes.
Confucius said, Whoever plays the music
controls the world, spinning like a top
on the palm of his hand. (He ordered the killing
of 80 musicians.) Elder Brother said,
"*My* elder brother of Boston went
back just this morning. He's upset
over his kids. Every one of them married
a white demon." He laughed a big, relishing
laugh, not the laugh that Chinese
make after telling a tragic awfulness. I

translated for Earll, "A generation of nephews
and nieces married white demons!" Elder
Brother looked at my husband, did a double-
take—a white demon! He saw me laughing,
and gave 2 thumbs up, and cheered, "Okay!"
Thumbs up with strong farmer's hands.
He and Earll walked hand in hand
through the fields. I stayed with the women—
our families have many more girls
than boys—and watched the 2 men now giant,
human, against sky and land, now
as nothing, transitories in the infinite.

To amble the earth that you work daily is to give
yourself and your guest entertainment and rest.
Earll understood his Elder Brother-
in-Law to be naming his happinesses. Ah,
generous fields of rice. Ah, great
water buffalo, and baby buffalo. Ah,
kinship. But for skin dark from the sun,
and arms and legs brawny from labor, this "brother"
looked like my real American brothers. None
of the women looked like my sisters and mother.
In Earll's presence, they marveled, "He doesn't
understand us. We can say anything
we want." They dared one another,
"Say whatever you like to say." I listened
hard, but didn't catch their secrets. I saw
the brick stove where my mother cooked,
reading a novel all the while, and let
the food burn. She'd foraged for straw
to heat that stove. I saw my parents' cupboard
bed. She snatched the curtain that she'd embroidered—
the marriage of Phoenix and Dragon, and "Good Morning"
in English script—and fled. My last Chinese
journey, a year and a half ago, the new
superhighway from Guangzhou to my villages—

4 hours. No more stopping for farmers
threshing grain and sun-drying fruit
and vegetables on the fine strips of new road.
I opened the car door; a man looked in.
I gazed, looking for the familiar; I watched
his gaze adjust, brighten. We recognized
each other, older—Elder Brother,
Younger Sister. Leading the welcoming crowd,
we walked through the village. "I've just been
elected president," he said, "voted in
for the second time president of the Old People's Hui."
Some old men sat in chairs along

a sunny wall. Elder Brother presented them,
"The Old People's Hui. Our clubhouse."
Red paper announced names of donors,
all Hongs, all Americans, and the plan
to build a bench, right there, over
the mud and trash hole. Of course,
our village would choose Elder Bro the leader;
he's energetic, optimistic, like me,
like most of our family, who give public
service (though shy and rather be private).
In war, he'd be the one taken as headman.
The old women, 4 of them, sat on the earth

in the shade of a wall across the way. They'd
played here as girls, and now rest,
still friends, laughing, remembering. They look
like homeless street people in the United States;
Chinese, maybe Chinese-American,
women, old like these women, clad
like them, faded pants and shirts, hair
home-cut, bobby-pinned back from
their ears, such women are scavenging
garbage cans. They don't beg, don't
panhandle, only quietly delve
through public trash. I overheard a white
man tell his son, "People like that
shouldn't live." Elder Brother nudged me,
"Give lei see. Go ahead.
Give, la. Give, la. Give
to her; she's important. She's of
the Hui. Give to him too; he's important."
I bent over the fanny pack at my belly.
Please have enough. Gotta keep count,
save some for later farther journey.
MaMa's spirit took me over.
I am my mother, bent over my purse,
digging through the mess for lei see,

anxious that I'd forgotten it, lost it,
run out. Stolen. Not enough.
Old squirrel rummaging in her pouch,
counting how much to save, how
much to give away. Keeping track
who got lei see already. Worked so
hard for money; what's it for but to give
to family? But let me give lei see
gracefully. Not let worry show. The time
has come, the occasion is rightnow that I saved
for, saved red paper, saved clean
new bills, artfully folded the money,
creased edges, tucked flaps. Carry
lei see with you wherever you go,
be ready to give it away. Aha. Whew.
Here's the secret compartment, here's lei see.
Take out just so many, keep
enough for descendants of second and third wives
in Mother's village. *Lei see dai gut*
to you. And you. You too.
You're welcome. Most very welcome. Thank *you*.
You prosper too. You *do* prosper.
People showed me their cell phones; last
visit, they showed me PVC

pipes. The inside of my ancestral home
was changed, the dirt floor covered, tiled.
Earth indoors no more.
Chickens used to peck the dirt clean,
and kitties played, and cats warmed themselves
by the stove. That brick stove that my mother re-
built, and cooked at. Read novels while cooking.
Food burned, and her mother-in-law scolded.
On my earlier visit, a pig had peered in at us,
forehoof taking a step inside,
but decided, too crowded, too many
noisy people, stepped back, and left.
This visit, I didn't see a chicken,
duck, goat, or cat, or pig in the house
or lanes and alleys. A TV sat
to the side of the altar; the symmetrical array
of emblems, calligraphy, and family photos that took
up the center of the wall faced the front door.
You walk in, and the first thing you see,
all you see, is altar up into the loft.
I have entered my playhouse. The last
time I was here, it was not so obvious
that my family kept a shrine. But then they
were concluding the 10 years of Great Calamity,

the Great Proletarian Cultural Revolution,
and the altar was plain, a mere outline,
a space framed with red paper. The light
bulb was hung before it. No icons
nor idols but family photos. Us.
"Which sister are you?" "This is me;
I'm the eldest sister." I'd gone to the other
end of the earth, and found pictures of myself;
they'd been thinking of me. The altar now
was resplendent with words inkbrushed on fresh
red paper. Elder Brother and his wife,
Elder Sister, sat beside my husband

and me on a row of chairs and stools along
the altar, our backs to it. Other relatives sat
to the sides, as in the inglenook back home.
Seats were covered with patterned fabric,
which decorated the altar too. Everybody
talked, said that he or she was happy,
life was good, all was well. The many
people not here, also well.
(Rude and bad luck to state otherwise.)
Ah, here come 2 cousins home
from the army. They've been gone all day
at their job, and are home from work. The Chinese

army is not like your American army;
they are boy scouts, do good
deeds, give help. My soldier cousins,
being young men preoccupied with making their way,
making their lives, were not much interested
in me, some old relative. Mumbling,
they shook hands because I stuck out
my hand. Elder Brother said to me,
"Greet our grandma and grandpa, la."
Amid the people, my people, there sat
on a little bench a bowl of incense
in sand. "Up there. Ah Po and
Ah Goong are up there." I stood
to look where he pointed. My grandparents
are up in the loft? Their ashes? Their ghosts?
Above the altar? Up higher than the loft?
In heaven? Someone handed me a stick of incense.
Earll was beside me, also with lit incense.
In unison, holding the stick like the stem of a flower
between prayer palms, we raised it toward
the ancestors, bowed, bowed again, bowed
the third requisite bow—I felt at my back
a heat, a wind, a spirit, blow in
through the open door—and planted the incense

in the sand. Thank god for Zen practice.
I had not lost li, though gone to the West.
They had not lost li—tradition,
manners, the rites—though Cultural Revolution.
I asked to see the water buffalo.
"We saw the baby buffalo last time.
Is he still with you?" Yes, oh yes.
Again, my family, followed by people all
along the way, people somehow also
family, walked through the lanes and alleys
of the village to muddy paths that went past
a dump pile. Elder Brother apologized,

"So dirty." I said, "It's okay."
I compost. What shocked me was the bits
of plastic trash mixed in with the leaves,
peelings, manure, and earth. Reds and blues
that do not occur in nature. Not a flower
in sight. My family are practical farmers;
they don't plant ornamentals. We entered
a huge old structure of stone and brick.
Foliage, small trees, grew inside,
up toward the broken roof and blue sky.
There, tethered to a column—long rope
from ionic base to nose ring—was

the water buffalo, grown, immense, dark.
Great curved, ridged, backward swooping,
sharp-pointed horns. "Lai, la.
Lai, la." With one hand, Elder
Brother gestured come, come closer;
his other hand had ahold of the nose ring
controlling the water buffalo's head. A swing
of its head, a stomp of a hoof, we're goners. It
was uneasy; it didn't like being pulled
into a commotion of visitors. And cameras flashing,
taking pictures of the city cousin and cousin-
in-law bumbling into country life.
Pet-pat it—where? on the nose?

the face? the shoulder? What if it swung about
to look at what touched it? I tried
sending it friendly thoughts. Remember me?
I remember you. You were a baby
with big long soft ears that stuck
out, like your horns stick out now.
I love your deep bright eyes, and eyelashes.
So, this is the animal that doorgunners chased
from helicopter gunships, and shot
to pieces. *"His balls explode, and I watch
that two thousand pound creature jump*

ten feet off the ground. . . . Everybody
laughs."—John Mulligan, Viet Nam veteran.
It had happened just south of here, not long ago.
I'm sorry, Buffalo. I am sorry.
I asked, "What is this place?" This ruin.
The columns. The dais. The faded red words
on the still-standing walls and on the column
that staked the buffalo. I make out
the word *moon.* The word *live.* The word
teacher. I know too little Chinese.
"This place was the old temple. The typhoon
wrecked it." His free hand—he wore a watch,
a silver watch—pointed to the broken walls,
and roof that let in swaths of sky. "Home
for my buffalo now." So, is this what's become
of the Hong temple? Are those the steps where
the guys hung out and teased the girls, and made
my mother drop her water jar, which broke,
and she got a scolding? Is this the same temple
I'd seen them restoring after Cultural
Revolution? The one we sent money for
changing back from a barn? The Communists banned
religion; temple became barn. The typhoon
had wrecked the old temple. Or were
Red Guards the Typhoons? I had gleefully

sent money; I would make my own cultural
revolution—get the names of women,
women donors, up on the temple walls,
and change the patrilineage. The literate villagers
deciphered for me the time-faded, white-
washed red writing on the column and walls:

> Great Teacher
> Great Leader
> Great Commander-in-Chief
> Great Helmsman
> Long Live Chairman Mao
> Conservation of Electricity
> Production Safety

I was hoping for something from the Tao
and Confucius. Maybe, beneath layers of paint:

> Farmers
> farm
> all the way to
> heaven.

"See the trees?" said Elder Brother, extending
his arms toward the surounding grove, branches

sticking through the roof, branches through
the walls. "I planted each tree. With extra
money, I buy a small tree. I'm growing
forest. I'm a planter of forests." He must
have been planting all his life; those are
grandmother-size trees looking in on us.
"Do you own this land, these fields?"
"The government took land and fields." "No,"
said another relative, so quietly, only
I heard, "the government gave land back."
Every story you hear, you will hear its opposite.
"Did you know our grandmother?

Do you remember Ah Po?"
"Ho chau!" Very mean, a scold.
He told: "I cared for Ah Po the last
5 years of her life. She lay in bed,
shouting for me, and I helped her." He must've
been a kid too young for the fields.
I remember the photograph of Ah Po
lying on her side in her cupboard. Her hair
combed back tight, she was dressed in black,
and she wore shoes on her once-bound feet.
Before sending money, my parents had wanted
evidence that she was alive. What cost to find

and hire a cameraman, and what delay
until her picture reached us, and the money
reached her. It is my American karma,
I am behooved: Constantly send money,
the least we can do. A sweetness would pop
into my mouth; Ah Po was sending candy.
All my brothers and sisters felt it, all
at the same moment. "I cared for Ah Po,
and I cared for Chuck's first wife.
I gave care to 4 people." Chuck is
Elder Brother's elder brother, who left
for America, and married a Chinese American.
Chuck's the one, all his children married
white demons. First Wife requested,
Send me one of the sons; you have so many.
A son did write letters to her, in English
to be translated, addressing her as Dear Mother. But
she went mad from loneliness, and had to be taken
care of. He didn't say who the other 2
were he was caregiver to. Maybe Ah Goong, who
went to fight the Japanese, and came back
not right in the mind. All Grandfather's
generation, and Father's generation,
and the brothers of his own generation left

for the Gold Mountain, and put the old parents
and old wives into this farmer's
keeping hands. Elder Brother's name is:
Benefit the Nation, like the motto that Yue Fei's
mother tattooed on his back. Be
constant sending money, the least we can do.
Letting go of the buffalo, Elder Brother said,
"Lai, la. Lai, la. Come,
come see the new temple." We hurried
back through the village. The temple, holding
the east side of the plaza, looked as I'd seen
it 23 years ago. Up high,

on the tympanum:
one big word, *Hong. Soup.*
It looks important, and it looks funny.
The first king of the first dynasty was named Soup.
So the oracle bones say. In famine,
in illness, slow-boil in water: leaves and bark
and grasses, scraps, whatever everybody has.
(Never the seeds for planting.) Drink soup,
be well. The water for making life-
saving soup came from this well
beside me, this well centered in the village
square, this well in front of the temple.
My aunt killed herself, and she killed the baby,

in this well. I looked down into it,
but did not see a very deep hole,
did not see the eye that reflects stars.
The water came to the top of the well; it seemed
to be drawn up through porous stone but
inches away, ankle-deep. My aunt
with the baby couldn't possibly have jumped into
a well this shallow, and drowned. A crone,
wee, shriveled to my size, gripped
my hand tight in her hand, which was cold
and clammy. She said, "You and I
are very related." We are ho chun.
I thought, Don't touch me; I don't want
to catch your disease. I felt her hard bones
around my wrist, my arm. In her other
hand was a bowl of water. She let go of me,
and with both hands offered me water.
Water from the well. Her hand was cold
and wet because of clear, clean well
water. I touched the water, as cold as
though iced. I touched it with both hands, put
both hands into the water, then
touched my forehead, touched my eyes,
and held my palms against my cheeks, held
my face in my hands. I am blessing myself,

and my aunt, and all that happened.

Earll did as I did, the crone standing before him,

proffering the bowl of water. On this hot

day, we did not drink; the water

was not meant for us to drink. The crowd

was not looking at us, when a Chinese crowd

will gather and look at anything, watch who

wins the haggling, watch the street barber

cut hair, watch anybody write anything.

The villagers were looking away, knowing, we

had shame, we had curse. They gave us privacy.

Gave us face. Are they wondering whether I

am wondering, Do they know? Do they know

that I know? The crone woman—now

where is she?—is she old enough

to've witnessed the raid on our house? The people

at the old folks' club, had they taken part?

Killing the animals, hounding my aunt. The men.

One of those men her rapist, her lover?

She gave birth in the pig sty. She drowned,

and the baby drowned in this very well.

Are these things ever past? Kids saw.

Can you ever get over it? Sex, bad.

Birthing, bad. Woman, bad. So,

lifetimes later, a strange old lady

brings to me and my husband a bowl
of water. She holds it in her 2 hands.
Chinese will serve ordinary tea
with the attention of both hands. I hope
she means to be making ceremony; I shall
take it to be shriving. The bad we did
be over. Punishment be over. Suffering be over.
Is that it then? Wet my hands in the well
water—the bowl like the well, and my wet face
like my sinful aunt's. Perhaps the well water
is being offered innocently, I the only one
who remembers the past, and believes in history's
influence. And believes ritual settles scores.
My husband by my side blessing himself as if
with the holy water of his youth stands in
for the rapist / lover. Forgiven. Curse lifted.
War over.

MOTHER'S VILLAGE

Let us be on our way.
"We drive to your mother's village, la."
Elder Brother climbed into the van, easily;
he's ridden cars often. He has a TV

set, a watch, cell phone, camera.
He farms with a buffalo. I hope
he doesn't feel poor, doesn't want
a tractor, a car. Maybe he's Green.
The nearest town, Gujing, calls
itself "Guangdong's First Green City."
And "China's First Green City."
May my family choose to farm with buffalo
rather than machinery, fully aware of bettering
the health of Planet Earth. Is Gujing
the same as Gwoo Jeng? Place names
on the map of China, if the way "home"
that MaMa taught us is on maps at all,
are nearly the sounds she had us memorize.
Gujing. Gwoo Jeng. We speak
a peculiar dialect. And language revolutions
have changed the spellings of cities and towns,
provinces, mountains and rivers. Villages never
on maps. Translating Chinese words
with other Chinese words, Mother
said that Gwoo Jeng means Ancient Well.
Or many Ancient Wells. We got to Mother's
village only 5 minutes away. In her day,
it was so far that her bridesmaids
teased her. "Marry a man from Tail End . . ."

We arrived at a third temple, adorned
and open as if for holiday. People, nicely
dressed, city style, with a television
crew, greeted us on its steps. "You missed
the festival. The ninth month, ninth day
festival. Just yesterday. Ten thousand
old people came. We fed
ten thousand old people." I was
late for Old People's Day; we in
the United States don't celebrate it, maybe
a Communist invention. And maybe only 100
or 1,000 came. In China, numbers are
mystical. 10,000 means many, many.
Multitudes. A countless number of old,
venerably old, lucky old people
came to my mother's village temple,
and were fed. But I was here before;
this place had not been a temple.
It had been the music building. I loved
the dichotomy: Father's ground was sacred,
Mother's, profane. 23 years ago,
I stood in front of a cement bunker-like
structure shut, it seemed, since my mother
left for America. In there, MaMa
and her villagers banged drums and blew horns,

banged and blew all night of the eclipse,

until the frog let go of the moon. They made

musical offerings night after night when

the witch's broom, Halley's comet, swept heaven.

But the broom would not leave the sky.

So, kingdoms rose, kingdoms fell.

So, world wars. I stood in front

of the wood door, which no one thought to open

for me, and I did not think to ask. Children

played on the paved entranceway, and in

the stream that flowed beside the music building.

Chinese and Vietnamese make music

on the water for that amplitude of sound.

The kids, likely kin to me many

times removed, paid me no mind.

Backing up, I read the name of Mother's

village above the door: 5 Contentments

Earthfield. And backing up farther,

I saw in green cursive: Music Meeting.

The words seemed green jade embossed

on white jade. The tablet was set in the fret-

work of a balcony. My father wrote beneath

the photo I took:

5 Contentments Earthfield Music Meeting Ting

A ting is a pavilion. A ting is the vessel for cooking
offerings at altars and at banquets. Ting Ting,
my name, like pearls falling into a jade bowl
bell, like worlds spinning in the palm of the hand.
Warm evenings when the Music Meeting was dark,
my mother's father had sat right here
where I'm sitting now, on the dirt ground
of this very patio, and talked story.
"Your grandfather talked stories so good
to hear, he made old ladies cry."
I'm an old lady myself now, come
to China, where old ladies live long,
see everything. Too tough to die.
What could make a hard old lady cry?
"Orphans. Mother dying, father dying
sing advice to their lone child how to
live without them: 'You'll never see me again,
not in this form. And I'll not see you,
nor look after you, nor feed you anymore.
Only notice now and then: When you walk
out the door, and a breeze touches you,
it's me touching you. Flowers I was wont
to plant will pop up in spring; they're me,
happy to be with you. And the flowers that come
out in fall—chrysanthemums—me, again!

And once a month, look for your father,
Jack Rabbit cooking medicine in the full moon.
See him? See his tall ears, slanting
to the right? See his cauldron? Father! *Joy kin!*'"
Joy kin is our village way of saying
zaijian, see again, au revoir.
The orphan, grown, sings: "I feel
the breeze at the open door, I feel
the breeze at the gate. Mother? I feel
a tap on the back of my neck. Ghost Mother?
A snow pea, a green finger, bounding
on its vine, touched me. *Joy kin. Joy kin.*"

Sit very still, and you will feel
the ancestors pull you to earth by a bell rope
that ties you—through you—from underground to sky.
They pull downward, and pull heavenly energy
down into you, all your spirited self.
They let up, and life force geysers out
from your thinking head and your hardworking hands.

My first visit to my mother's village, my mother
still living then, I looked for her house
among the gray-with-mildew houses, walked
through the mazy lanes saying her name.

Brave Orchid. No flowers, no color
but in girls' names. Do you know the family
of Brave Orchid? Doctor Brave Orchid,
who gave shots against smallpox.
A woman and a boy, far cousins, were waiting
for me at the raised threshold of a wide-
open door. She said, Good to see you.
I said, Good to see you. "Ho kin."
"Ho kin." She did not give her name.
I did not give my name. We
had to talk about how we were related;
we would find kin names to call
each other. She is married to my mother's
brother's son. I am the oldest daughter
of her father-in-law's oldest daughter.
I wanted to call her Sister, but Elder Sister?
Younger Sister? I couldn't tell whether
she were older or younger than me. Her hair
was black, her skin dark and lined, some teeth
gone. Besides, her father-in-law was not
really my mother's brother. He was son
of the third wife; my mother was daughter
of the first wife. My grandfather, the one
who sat in the square and told the stories

that made old ladies cry, the grandfather
who could do anything, make wine, make
tofu, make cheesy fu ngoy
that stunk up the house, the grandfather
who was judge of the village, that grandfather
sailed the world, and brought home wives.
The third wife, whose skin was black, whose
jabber no one understood, he brought
from Nicaragua. The boy cousin-how-
many-times-removed standing before me,
looking at me, did seem very dark-skinned,
but he plays out in the tropical sun all day.

The dark woman living in my mother's house
did not invite me inside. I peeked
behind her, and saw a courtyard that looked
like a roofless work and storage room. Most
of it was taken up by piles of straw. MaMa
said that she spent most of her day
foraging the hills for straw. They use it to kindle
the stove, which was in a corner, gray bricks
blackened with cooking smoke. Laundry—blue
pants, blue shirts, one white shirt—
hung on bamboo poles eave to eave.
It's clothing that gives the gray village color.

Partway across and up a roofline,
atop clay tiles, shaped on their makers'
thighs, were a row of jade-like figures—
dogs? lions? faeries? kachinas?—maybe
broken, maybe never finished. Extra
bamboo of various lengths stood
against a wall. A wooden stick, milled,
no nodes, no knots, was fastened
across a shut door, high enough
for a person to walk under upright.
On the heavy wood door were posted 2 words:
Family Something. Family Living Room?
Family Forbidden? News had come to us
that this uncle could not pay taxes,
so the government forbade the use of a room.
Don't let up sending money.
My grandfather had no business being
a trigamist. Poverty for generations. I
looked as far as I could see into
the house, and saw a doorway beyond a doorway
beyond a doorway. A little boy in red
was looking at me from a faraway dimension.
The men of my mother's family were hiding. They
were afraid that I, eldest daughter of eldest

daughter of First Wife, had come to take possession
of house and land. As I handed the dark woman
and the dark boy many red envelopes
of money (may she distribute it fairly), I said,
"All the turmoil, the not-good, that MaMa
tells me about you—it's over. No more.
I'll send money. I won't forget. I shall
send you money forever."

                            But I do forget. Years
go by when I don't send money, enough
money. I forget China; I forget my family there.
China is too far away. I need
to think it up. I need a time machine.
To imagine hard to make real the people
who appear in letters, stories, dreams, how
to get to them. They forget me too;
I am forgotten. They rarely write
reminding me, Send money. We, all of us,
fall into forgetfulness. Sammosa.
I should've said to my Nicaraguan relatives:
You take the house. You keep the land.
House and land, yours. I give you this house.
I give you this property. But I didn't think
it was mine to give. Who knows who owns

the estate. The collective farm? The Communist

government? Maybe it already belongs

to my enate people. It would've done my Nicaraguan

sister good to hear me say, Here,

it's all yours.

              Now, when I arrived

again in my mother's village, the day after

Old People's Day, 9/9,

no one of that side of my family was there at

the music temple to welcome me. Not the dark woman,

not any relative with the same grandfather

as me, not one of the men descended

from my step-step-grandmother from Nicaragua.

Who greeted me and shook my hand was the mayoress,

skirt-suited like a woman politician in the West.

She'd be the one in charge if invaders came.

Not the headman, like the president of the seniors,

not the storyteller, like my grandfather.

The mayoress led me, and her assistants, and Earll,

and a couple of Roots officials, and some teachers

and translators, and a TV crew with camera

and mike up the stairs and through the thrown-

open doors. The inside of the temple

was adazzle with light. Impossible brightness that was not

coming from windows or lightbulbs. All
shining, squares and diamonds of fresh red
paper on walls and tabletops shining,
black writing on the red, shining. The villages
grew out of old dark earth;
mold and dust, motes and motes of time,
blacken the adobe and gray the air. Air
pollution hazed the sun; this day
will not count as a blue-sky day.
And yet, the music temple was a surround of light.
The templekeepers had not cleaned up
after the feast of Old People's Day.

The small chairs, some on their sides,
had not been put away. 10,000
people couldn't've fit. The old folks
ate, were honored in shifts. They'd come
walking, riding on the backs of their children,
riding bicycles, rowing boats, come
here from all over Pearl River
delta. Someone handed me a lit stick
of incense. I, followed by the crowd curious
to see whether this daughter who'd been gone
so long knew and kept the ways—li—
walked step by mindful step toward

the altar, which was the entire back wall.
Holding the stick of incense between palms,
I bowed thrice. 1 goak goong.
2 goak goong. 3 goak goong.
Learned in childhood in Stockton, California.
Maybe means: First, nourish grandfather.
Second, nourish grandfather. Third,
nourish grandfather. Big downbeat
bow on 3. I bowed and bowed and bowed
to ancestors arraying the back wall and
side walls. 18 ancestors,
each dated with years consecutively
from 960 to 1279.

They wore the high headdresses of high
rank. They had my mother's name: Chew.
Next to *Chew* was a simple word that I
had asked my mother to draw, giving me
the name of the kings in the stories she told.
Almost blind, she'd written that word.
I asked the mayoress, "Please say this word."
"Sung." She touched both words.
"Chew Sung." She swept her arm right to
left across the altar. "The Chew Sung
huang dai." *Kings. Emperors. Gods.*

"Ten thousand old people bowed to them."
From the last (1271–1279)
emperor's picture, the genealogy tree
continued along the left wall to the door.
"Your names are here," said the mayoress, pointing
to branches nearest the door. A fear
went through me, that fear when I am about
to learn something. I asked carefully,
"Were we soldiers? Were we servants?"
I would've asked, "Were we courtiers?"
but didn't know *courtier*. Most likely,
we were courtiers. "No! No! You emperor!

You emperor!" You who left for America,
became American, you forget everything.
You forget who you are. Emperor!
Chew Sung Emperor. Emperor of the Northern Sung.
Emperor of the Southern Sung. A teacher of English
took my hand, bowed over it, and said,
laughing, "Your majesty." So, the stories
about mighty sea battles, gunpowder bombs,
lost wars, 100,000
refugees, the boy emperor falling
off the typhoon-broken ship,
the other boy emperor tied to the back

of the prime minister, the Lum woman who hid

the princes, passed the young dragons off

as "Big Lum" and "Little Lum"—"Forever,

you meet a Lum, you carry her shoes"—

the mass suicide of queens and princesses

at the river, the stone you can see today

to remember the last, lost battle, "Sung"

carved on one side, "Yuan" the other,

and more stones, the Empress's Dressing Table

Stone and the Throne Stone—all that history,

us. We were the carriers of the Traveling Palace;

wherever we settle, that's the Center.

Kuan Fu, the long-lost capital,

is *here*. Found. The Traveling Palace was built

of mud and straw, rocks for furniture. My father

teased my mother, "You lived like Injuns."

Their stories of the Sung were always about its fall,

the trauma of war, the running as refugees.

The conqueror was Yuan. (I'd thought, Juan in Cuba.

"Cousin Juan threw away BaBa's

poems. Juan stole the book box.")

The Yuan are Mongols, and their leader was Kublai Khan.

I had to research for myself the glory of Sung.

Sung was the age when the ecosystem was healthiest.

From atop the Great Wall where now you see loess,
you would've gazed out at forests of elm,
planted as the Great Wall was being built.
Women were teachers; they even taught their sons
military strategy. General Yue Fei
and his mother were Sung. The Sung mapped the land
and the sky. Its navy patrolled the rivers and seas.
(But the Yuan had a larger navy; the Mongol
women fought on horseback and on warships.
The Sung deforested the Xiang River Valley
for wood and metal to build ships and to forge
weapons.) Movable type was invented during Sung,
and paper money. And the compass: they discerned true
north. Artists made Buddhas and bodhisattvas.
There was a poet named Poet. Poet
wrote about travels that take but a day
then home again. Painters painted the long
journeys. The long golden handscroll,
"18 Songs for Barbarian Reed Pipe":
Nomads capture Wen-chi, poetess
and composer, daughter of the librarian. She
is the barbarians' treasure, taken from her home
of many roofs and courtyards. She rides
a dappled horse escorted by processions of men

on dark horses and camels across the yellow
grass of the steppes and yellow sands of the desert.
They play flutes as they ride. Hooves of the horses
beat percussion. The earth is drum. Falcons
ride on shoulders and wrists. She sees migrating
geese make words in the sky; she reads them as letters
from home. She pricks her finger, and writes with blood
a message from her heart. "Let my heart
be heard from the ends of the earth." The wild geese
can read words written in the blood of a loyal one's
heart, and fly them to those who wait to hear.
The nomads, Liao people, women and men,
girls and boys fight, hunt, play

with crossbows and longbows and arrows.
They gallop their horses under the geese, and shoot
them down. Birds become afraid of people.
"I want to kill myself. I am among
nonhumans. I want to kill myself.
I am a prisoner with ten thousand anxieties
but no one to confide them to. I want to kill
myself. I have to make finger gestures,
yes, no. I have no speech.
I want to kill myself. The barbarian
with a pretty face wants to make me his wife.

I will kill myself. Yes, I shall.
I am pregnant with a barbarian child.
I shall kill myself." At her wedding to the prince
of barbarians, musicians play pipa,
horn, and flute. They have 2 sons, half
Liao, half Han. An envoy comes bearing
ransom. The covered wagon with red wheels
is waiting to carry her home. The nomads stand
in groups and alone, and weep into their long sleeves.
Wen-chi, wife and mother, holds
her baby for the last time. Her husband, whom she
has learned to trust, holds their son by the hand.

The children do not understand to weep.
Liao horsemen and Han horsemen and infantry
in procession escort Wen-chi's return.
Husband and sons, elder son on his own
small horse, the baby carried in a rider's
lap, accompany her partway. The prince
rides his wife's dappled horse, saddled
with snow-leopard fur. He constantly looks
back at her wagon, which is drawn by 2 oxen
with up-growing horns. The scroll ends
at the home with many roofs and courtyards.
But now people are everywhere, enjoying themselves,

the streets alive, the teahouse open; the baker
sells buns to the returning soldiers;
kids walk with their mothers and fathers.
And the house comes to life as Wen-chi
goes up the stairs toward her kinswomen;
one kowtows to her; the rest shrink
away from her, cover their mouths with long sleeves.
They are protecting themselves from her strangeness.
Wen-chi will help her father compile
a new library.
   My father wrote
that her legend reminds him of 2 prisoners,
Su Wu and Li Ling. In 100 B.C.,
during the thousand-year war, Su Wu,
ambassador to the Mongols, went to their country
to negotiate for peace. The Khan poisoned him, beat
him, kept him from leaving the desert. His labor
was to herd sheep to grass and water. Meanwhile,
in battle against the Mongols, Li Ling surrendered.
He was a valuable P.O.W.
because he could be forced to write letters
to Su Wu, and influence him to favor the enemy.
The 2 men carried on their correspondence
for 19 years, on paper and by wild goose.

"No matter I am in a foreign land.
No matter the hardship. My heart that loves
is always with Mother Earth / Land, China."
My father wrote on the margin of my writing
on Wen-chi:

> Su Wu
>
> Li Ling
>
> My biographies

I feel so bad. BaBa
lived in the Americas for over 60 years—

left for Cuba as a teenager, not
meaning to be gone forever—and never became
at home anywhere. *He* was a prisoner of barbarians. I
should've brought him with me to China. I'd gone
10, 12 times (counting Taiwan,
counting Hong Kong), but never thought
to ask him to come along. Because his papers
were fake. He was an illegal alien. We should've
chanced going, if only to join for a while
the hosts and hosts of people whose joy it is
to be a crowd walking along the river.

. . .

Without Father, without Mother, I traveled
to China, the Central Nation, and found out
that I myself am Empress of the Center. I
was bowed to; I was addressed "Your majesty."
I walked down the steps of the music temple.
I walked with the crowd, my people, along
a stream of Pearl River and time. I felt
the crowd full; they are all here—Wen-chi
and her retinues, Fa Mook Lan and her army,
the Vietnamese princess and her
celebrants, Chu Ping and the dragon boat
racers, the Long Marchers, John Mulligan
and the shopping cart soldiers, and old people

from long ago and from yesterday. All
these people belong to me. The ground
I'm walking belongs to me. I feel ownership
of the fields before me, and the hills I see and the hills
beyond my sight, and the river and the connecting rivers
to the South China Sea, and the Indian Ocean, and more
oceans, and lands the waters touch. I own
and am responsible for all of it. My kuleana.
My duty. My business. Up to me. I walk
my land and territory, and see how, what
my people are doing. I've felt this majesty before—
at Cal Berkeley, my university, where I studied

and taught. I walk that campus of groves and daylight
creeks, and hills, whence I watch the sun
set into the horizon and compassing sea.
Mine: the Lawrence Berkeley National Laboratory,
the Radiation Laboratories, the ones in Livermore
and Los Alamos. And the cyclotron and the stadium,
both sitting on the Hayward Fault, on the North
American Plate crunching past the Pacific Plate.
My failure: U.C. Berkeley sawed down
and wood-chipped the oak grove and Grandmother Tree.
The next task: Prevent British Petroleum,
which endowed 50 million dollars to Cal, from
building labs along—over—Strawberry
Creek and up and across Strawberry Canyon.

Jingyi, the English teacher who recognized
me—"your majesty"—teaches at Jinan
University. MaMa had a friend
who taught there, visited us in California;
I couldn't find her at Jinan, moved to Australia.
I took Jingyi's hand. Holding hands,
laughing, we walked from the music temple, walked
along the river, walked with our village.
(Ours, though she's from Xinjiang, where Uighurs live.)

I joined, a day late, the 10,000

old people. And the crowd walking

jam-packed along the Red River in Viet Nam

(Red River too in Minnesota) and the Perfume

River through Huế. And the lines of mourners reading

the names on the Vietnam Memorial, and seeing

ourselves, like a platoon, like a peace march, reflected

in the black granite. Crowdstream everywhere

always walking, moving, moving, migrating,

connecting, separating, losing the others, off

on one's own, finding them, losing them again,

finding again. We are a curl of the scroll,

"Along the River during Ching Ming Festival."

People dressed in holiday clothes are leaving

their huts and villas, crossing bridges on foot

and on horses and camels, rowing little boats

along the banks and around islands and shoals.

Ladies are riding sedan chairs from out

the city gates. Men work the festival,

selling food and tree branches, juggling

balls and plates, staging a play, staging

a puppet show. Men carry loads.

Men drive wide teams of mules,

10 mules wide. Poor men beg;

monks beg. Mid-river, mid-scroll,
the Rainbow Bridge carries people and animals
up and over the river. Oh. Oh.
A ship is blowing sideways into the bridge;
sailors are lowering the sails as fast as they can.
Teams of men on the shore and under the bridge
are pulling on tow ropes. A few people
at the railings watch for the ship to slide beneath them.
I remember: I was one of many tiny people—
the grown-ups tiny as well as the children—
walking through blue space, nothing
above and below but sky. We were refugees
fleeing war, carrying babies, carrying
bundles of all we own, herding and leading
work animals and pets, yet we were
happy and gay, dressed in layers and layers
of our prettiest clothes, out for a walk
on a bright and sunny day. Warm sun
lit scarves and blankets red and turquoise,
colors everywhere. I looked down
at my feet; I was wearing high-ankle shoes
of white light. I was walking on a floor
that was gold-brown skin, the back of a giant,
who had made a bridge of himself. His hands held

on to an edge of a mountain crevice, and his toes
dug into the opposite edge. My father
walked alongside me. I was safe;
I was not scared. I have a sure memory
of this scene of my life, but could it be
memory of a dream, a former incarnation, a movie?
I have searched high and low through archives
of movies, and cannot find the Rainbow Bridge
Giant helping people like my family and tribe
walk across the sky. I found proof
of happenings which I have no bodily nor
mental memory of—snapshots of me
riding a camel, sitting on a red and gold
blanket between its humps, riding on a cold
windy clear day atop the Great Wall.
Behind me and before me, the Great Wall
rises and falls, rises and falls with the domes
and kettles of the Qilian mountain range,
crenellated spine of Dragon. Guard towers
at interval peaks. With mittened hands,
I am tufting and petting the tawny liony fur
on the hump in front of me. The camel's hair
and my hair are blowing in the Gobi wind.
My hair—salt-and-pepper hair, not

long ago—blows across my face
and into my eyes. I should've said out loud,
and so remember, "I am astride a camel;
we're traveling the Long Wall. We'll take the Long Wall,
then the Silk Road, and arrive in the West."
As Empress of the Center, I see from on high:
all/no space and time, human
populations and individuals forever
on the move, migrating like bears and whales
and cranes, walking, riding, flying along
and across rivers and oceans, islands and continents.
"You twain! and all processions moving

along the streets! I wish to infuse myself among you
till I see it common for you to walk hand in hand."
I rented a bicycle, left my passport
as collateral, and joined a river of bicyclists.
Entering, merging, I pedaled, glided apace
in the steady, balanced surge of fellow cyclers.
Bells *burr burr-ring burr-ring*.
I wheeled along with families of 4, 5,
couples, babies with net over their faces,
high-heeled ladies, pets (an illegal puppy
peeked out of a box), poultry, furniture,
produce. All streaming along, streaming

on and on, rolling through intersections,
through markets, past pancake and corn-
on-the-cob venders, street barbers, podiatrists,
bicycle repairers, through the clink clink
clink of women breaking up rocks,
past the stadium, site of mass executions,
swooping left turns in front of honking
trucks, taxis, oncoming rivers
of other bicycles. Pulling, drafting, we flow.
We are blood. No moving over
to a curb, no getting off. Give in
to being lost; ride to unknown parts,
until the cycling mass lets me go.

Once I was on an airplane beside
a village girl in the window seat. At takeoff
I asked her, "Where are you going?"
"Waw!" She shouted in surprise, and grabbed
ahold of my hand, "You speak like me!"
"Yes, I speak Say Yup language."
"Are you from the village?" "No, my MaMa
and BaBa came from Say Yup villages.
They left for New York. They lived in New York,
then California. I was born in California."

I feel like a child, younger than this girl; I'm
telling about parents as if I still had them;
I'm talking in my baby language. "Waw!"
she exclaimed, loud as though yelling across fields.
"*I am going to New York! I*
am meeting my husband in New York. He's
waiting for me in New York. He works
in a restaurant. He's rented a home. He sent
for me, and waits for me." She did not
let go of my hand; I held hers tightly
as we flew the night sky. She looked
in wonder at webs of lights below.

"Red red green green," she said.
"Red red green green," my mother
used to say, meaning, Oh, how pretty!
The lights were white and yellow too, and gold,
blue, copper. And above, stars and stars.
Mother, MaMa, as you leave
the village family you'll never see again—
Grandfather walked her as far as he
could walk, stood weeping in the road until
she could not see him anymore when
she turned around to look. She's off to that lonely
country from where he returned broke—"I felt

that I was dying."—MaMa, girl,
you are not traveling alone. I am
traveling with you, here, holding your hand.
I know that country you're leaving for,
and shall guide you there. I know your future.
I'm your child from the future. Your husband
will certainly meet you. BaBa will
be at the East Broadway station.
You will recognize each other,
though he be dressed modern Western style.
You will have a good, good life.
You will have many children, and live a long,
long life. You will be lucky.
"You are lucky. Your husband has work.
He's rented an apartment, and made you a home.
He saves money. He bought your plane ticket,
he will be waiting for you at the airport."
She listened to the wise old woman teaching her.
But how to instruct anyone the way to make
an American life? How to have a happy
marriage? For a long time in the dark,
dozing, dreaming, thinking, we sat
without speaking, without letting go
of warm hands. The red red green

green appeared again. I told her,
"That's Japan. We're over Japan now.
We'll be landing soon in Narita."
"Waw! You speak Japanese too."
She admires me too much. Inside
the horrible confusion of the international
airport, how can a mind from
the village not fall to crazy pieces?
I found a nice American couple making
the connecting flight to New York, and asked
them please to take this Chinese girl
to the right gate. She thanked me. She said
goodbye, see you again. "Joy kin."
She did not look back. Good.
Gotta go, things to do, people
to meet, places to be.

CITY

                    I betook
myself to Xi'an. Like everyone,
I'm leaving village for city. But a city
so old and deep in-country, it has a chance

not to be the same global city
as every city. Xi'an means West Peace,
and was the capital during 4 eras, not Sung.
I stood at the bottom of the gray rock wall
of the walled city, looked up its slope,
looked to the curved sides, could not get
a sense of the whole layout. More solid
than Long Wall. A granite bowl banks
the earth around (parts of?) the city. I stood
on top of the wall, walked the boulevard
paved with bricks. I enjoyed spaciousness,
few walkers that day, few bicyclists.
At the ramparts on one side, I looked down
at ponds and moats. On the other side, sky-
scrapers, like a mirage city, much higher
than the walls. Relics of military defense,
walls are no barrier to attack, no
barrier to in-migration, never have been.
Xi'an, like the dusty villages, pushes out of
earth, and earth pulls it down into earth.
Build upward, towers, skyscrapers,
pagodas. Dig out of engulfing earth.
The air is dark. Everyone coughs.
Cover the kids' faces with gauzy scarves.

It's not just the cars. It's the wind
blowing sand into this city at the south-
easternmost edge of the Gobi desert.
The body of sand is shifting over eastward,
and uncovering rock ground. Down in the street,
though dirt gray (this day won't count
as blue-sky day either), glass
and steel shine through. Cities are full
of mirrors. My whole time in the villages, I
did not see a mirror. I had not looked
at my image. Village people live so close
together—everyone sees everyone every

day—they know how attractive or un-
attractive they are. Now the way I look
appears to me, here, there, in windows, on chrome,
in mirrors in markets and bathrooms. I have changed.
I am a dandelion puffball blur. My hair,
scribbles of white lines. My face. Lines
crisscross and zigzag my face.
My eyes. I am looking into eyes
whose color has turned lighter, hazy brown.
Wind and time are blowing me out.
The old women around me are vivid and loud.
Their hair is black. They're beggars, soliciting

in a group outside the temple, selling
incense and matches, but don't care whether
you buy or not. They're out of the house enjoying
ladies' company. A lone gray woman is
sitting on the curb by the crosswalk.
She's begging, not selling anything.
Begging is against the law. A policeman
and a cadre woman in charge of the street talk
to her for a long time. The cop kneels
to talk to her. She does not reply. I think
he's trying to convince her to cease begging,
to get up and move on. The cadre
woman, an old woman too, is not
giving her a scolding. They're treating her nicely,
speaking softly, secretively. They don't want
to make a scene on the street, don't want
this conturbation to be happening. Homeless old
beggar women? None such. I
keep watching. They won't hurt her as long
as the American tourist watches. After quite
a while, I have more interesting sights
to see, and leave. When I come back
to that street corner, she's gone. Why
is it that old women are China's refuse,

and men, war veterans, America's? When the society
is supposed to be honoring grandmothers, and admiring
macho men? "Do not let mother and father go
hungry; feed them meat from the flesh of your arm."
Walking past the incense ladies, all
acting important, I go inside the temple.
Up on platforms, the fortune-tellers,
all men, perform their specialties—
coins, yarrow, the I Ching, magic
birds, turtle shells. They read palms,
read the loops and whorls and arches on
fingerprints, read words on sticks of
bamboo, read faces and freckles
and bumps on heads. I buy a fortune.
I point to a little cage in a row
of little cages. The magic man slides
open the door. Out hops a java
finch. It picks up a card in its diamond
beak: the Woman Warrior, charging forth
on her white horse, wielding her double broadswords.
"You are brave, you will live a long life."
But he must tell everyone: You'll live long.
Never death. Never suicide. The java finch
eats a reward of seeds, and hops back

into its cage. In Xi'an, there are drum
towers and bell towers, and wild goose
towers. Chinese contrary, the Small
Wild Goose is 13 stories
high; the Big Wild Goose, 7.
A poet was once seen riding a wild goose,
flying over the city, and away. All
had been golden, the goose, the poet, his robes,
the towers. The eyewitnesses watched until
they saw what seemed to be a golden insect
vanish into the sky. I give incense
and make slow bows at Big Wild Goose,
that I should write well, like Du Fu
and Li Bai, who had both come here,
and written well. That my writing give life,
to whomever I write about, as Shakespeare
promised. Chinese are mad for long life.
Quest and wish for time, more time,
more, yet more. Carve poems and decrees
on rocks. Erect forests of steles. 500
pyramids to safeguard the emperors
inside them, and their armies, and horses,
acrobats, and musicians, always. I myself
have tasted longlife medicine—bitter.

My mother gave it to us. Rabbit-in-the-Moon—
my father—mixes the elixir for immortality.
But I have seen poets training in impermanence.
Early in the paved city, when dew beads
the marble and concrete, the poets write with water.
He or she stands quietly holding
the tall brush, like a lance, like a shuffleboard
paddle, like a pole vault pole. Then touches
the writing end—a cloth-wrapped mallet, not a mop—
down upon the hard ground, the page.
Legs spread, the poet, straddling the coming words,
sweeps downward stroke to the left, upward
stroke to the right, dabs quick dots,
pulls horizontal lines, pulls vertical
lines, flips a sharp-curve tail.
Gets to the end before the beginning dries.
Onlookers, readers, and fellow poets
leaning on their own writing poles, read
aloud the transpiring words, one
word, next word, then the whole
fleeting poem, exclaim over it, criticize it,
memorize it, sing it once more as the sun
dries it up. They stand around the spot
where the poem had been, don't step on it,

and discuss the writing of it, the idea of it,
the prosody of it with its creator. The sun rises,
time to wet the brushes in the water bucket.
Dip again and again, and write long
long lines. No corrections! No
reworking! One poet writes,
another poet writes—in answer!
I should've asked to borrow a writing pole,
and drawn an enso as big a circle as I
could make in one wet swoop all
the way around myself, me the center.
In Japanese Zen, on your 60th birthday,
you can draw a perfect circle. However
it arcs or squiggles, however black or faint,
large or small, one swoop or 2
discontinuous strokes—perfect.
You've brought to the making of it your lifetime
of ability. My perfect reader would know to read
my enso's journey from Asia to America back
to Asia, from classical times to modern, to New Age.
My writing fades, vanishes, ends. Okay.
In the park of formal gardens, the martial artists—
practitioners of the many ways of kung fu,
and disco, women with fans, women with the long
ribbon, swordswomen, swordsmen—are moving

and dancing to the rhythms of his own discipline,
her own discipline. Solitaries, too, claim
their places—the top of the round bridge,
the island of grass, the room behind a curtain
of weeping willow. Free to make whatever
expressions you like. Dance like nobody else.
I join this group and that one, get easily
into step, not worried, in sync,
out of sync, nobody's looking at me.
I'm part of the Chinese crowd. I stand
in first-position chi kung, and watch
the teacher direct her advanced students, who

have their backs to her. She waves her hands,
and they in unison leap into the air.
Waw! Wei! She's lifting, orchestrating
their jumps with chi. Her chi is mighty;
she is 90 years old. Teacher
walks up to me; she studies me.
I feel warmth from her eyes on my skin.
She adjusts my hands to make paws like
an upright-standing squirrel or bear.
She runs her hand straight down the center
of my chest. I feel power shoot
into me, heating my core, glowing. She'd

given me some of her chi, charged me with chi.
Chi is real; I am strengthened to this day.
"You stand for one hour," she says.
I stand for one hour. Marveling, there is such
a thing as chi. Yin wind, yang
wind, real. Life, love, soul,
good. And there are people who can
control it and transmit it, and teach you how
to acquire chi, and how to use it. At the end
of my hour, Teacher comes to check on me.
Her eyes scan me, land on my hair.
"Keep working on your chi kung;
your hair will turn black." Her hair
is jet-black. She doesn't like
white hair. I won't work chi kung
to change my hair; I want to change the world.
My body and mind taking on forms that
Chinese have been configuring for 4,000
years, my 12 meridians linking up
with the globe's 360, energy will round
the globe, and heal the bombed-up world.
I'm not alone; people here and people who've
migrated everywhere are doing this work of
influencing wind and water (feng shui).

We continue the life of the world. Live,
live, live, live.
                    In Xi'an,
there's a museum like the museum I made
as a kid for my collections, strange things
I picked up along the railroad tracks,
and in the slough, and in the cash register.
Deer hoof, a baby bat, counterfeit
money, fool's gold. Behind dusty
glass, there lay the arrow with nock-whistle
that I'd invented for the barbarians who
played the reed pipe. The poet's imagination
flies true. It works, it hit on the actual.
It can make up a thing that will
materialize, in China, in Time, the past, the future.
So, at the walled city of West Peace,
I come to the start of the Silk Road, which forks.
Southwest, the way Tripitaka Tang
and Monkey Sun Wu Kong went questing,
betakes you to India. Northwest, you'd end
up in Afghanistan, then Iran, then Uruk,
home of Gilgamesh—Iraq. Peace groups
invite me to these places, but I turn them down.
I don't want my heart to break.

Fa Mook Lan would go. She'd join
the army of whichever side held her family
hostage. She'd win battles, and receive
honorable discharge home, though the 1,000
years war is not done. Now
I know: She killed herself.
She had P.T.S.D.; her soldier's heart broke,
and she fell upon her sword. This month,
May 2009, more American soldiers died by
their own hand than killed by Iraqis and Al Qaeda.
So far this year, 62 suicides,
more than half of them National Guard;
138 in 2008. I have no words of consolation.

Wittman, son, brother, imaginary friend,
I need you. Help me again. Go
up Sky Mountain. Here, I'll
unwind for you a ribbon of rainbow silk
scrolling into golden desert. Walk
upon it with men in burnooses and women in burkas,
colors blowing and flapping, and camels swaying
and swinging bells, heading toward cities
and mirages of cities. The oasis that gives you
haven is Basra, the air station and naval

base. Basra, home of Sinbad the Sailor,
and before that, the Garden of Eden.
Please stand on a roadside, and hold
the Bell of Peace, a golden bowl, on
your proffering hand, and think this thought:
"Body, speech, and mind in perfect oneness,
I send my heart along with the sound of this bell.
May all the hearers awaken from forgetfulness,
and transcend the path of anxiety and sorrow."
Touch bell stick to bell, warming it,
breathe in, breathe out, then make one
sure stroke. The ring changes the air.

The ring rings through din. The din
stills. The ring makes silence all
around, all around. Explosions cease.
Bombardment ends. Combatants
stop to enjoy the sound of Buddha's voice.
The ring gathers time into one moment
of peace. Which is torn by engine noise
from a light, white aircraft, like an insect,
a whitefly. A drone. A hunter-killer drone.
Yell at it, "Coward! Coward!" We are cowards,
killing without facing those we kill,
without giving our victims a chance at us.

Yell "Coward" up at the drone,

then turn toward the air base and yell

at it, "Coward! Coward! Coward! Coward!"

Your voice carries all the way to Virginia,

where the computer specialist is pressing the buttons.

He hears you, wakes up, stops warring.

HOME AGAIN

Thank you, Wittman. Now go

continue on the Silk Road all the way

to its other end, in Soglio, where Taña awaits you.

It's Taña! My own dear wife.

Rush into each other's arms. Home.

No rancor. No ambivalence.

"I saw you constantly. I saw you everywhere."

True, blondes everywhere—Chinese

with yellow hair, natural and chemical—each

one startling—it's Taña. My heart leapt.

My heart fell—it wasn't you. "Welcome, Love.

Welcome back." The red string holds.

Hand in hand, the dear forever married

walk through the piazza with the bell tower,

and into the snow-topped mountains, stand
for a time on the Soglio mesa, and breathe
the good air between sky and far-down
chestnut forests. Rilke, who walked here,
advised, Change your life. Then westward
home, where Mario, one and only son,
has met his one true love, Anh Lan.
Please, no arguing, live happily ever after.

A long time has passed since I began
the journey of this poem. Poetry, which makes
immortality and eternity, does not stop

time. In 4 years real time:

MY DEAD
John Mulligan
Grace Paley
Pat Haines
Aunt Wai Ying Chew Lam
John Gregory Dunne and Quintana Roo
Ralph Swentzell
Jade Snow Wong
Vera Fessler
Irene Takei Miura
Roger Long

Phạm Tiến Duât

Roger Allsop

Carole Koda

Alyssa Merchant

John Griffin

Sandy Taylor

Ena Gibson

Stella Jue

Glenn Kawahara

Gene Frumkin

George Carlin

Guanfu Guo

Col. Kenneth En Yin Ching

Bob Winkley

Oakley Hall

Capitano

Marion Perkins

Kazuko Onodera

Laura Evelia Pérez-Arce Dávalos

Kristi Rudolph

Lawrence William Smith

Ardavan Daravan

Ian and Susan MacMillan

Michael Rossman

Auntie Nona Beamer

John Leonard

Eartha Kitt

Jim Houston

Mike Porcella

Ron Takaki

Eng Lay Dai Gwoo

Jerry Josephs

Naomi Gibson

Roy Colombe

Lucille Clifton

Dorothy Langley Hoge

Tom Pigford

Archie Spencer

Howard Zinn

Donovan Cummings

Henry Vallejo

Gloria Marie Bingesser Beckwith

Graham Nicholson

Charles Muscatine

Janet Adelman

Larry Feinberg

Jadin Wong

Ray Dracker

Jack Larson

Bob Nichols

Each one who dies, I want to go with you.
I feel your pull into death.
I want to join my dead.
I have broken the news that Fa Mook Lan
killed herself. Everyone who hears denies
that it happened. No. How? Why?
The woman soldier comes home from battle;
her child does not recognize his mother.
He cries at sight of her; he runs away from her.
Why not give up on life?
I found evidence, as scholars know evidence,
of how Fa Mook Lan died.
I was at a conference welcoming to Notre Dame
Bei Dao, the poet who wrote
a ritual for ending a thousand-year war.
The people kneel at an abandoned stone quarry,
and fly 50 paper hawks. In a footnote
of a paper entitled "A Poetic Lesson,"
I read that Fa Mook Lan killed
herself by hanging; she refused the emperor's
order that she become one of his wives.
The source cited was the P.R.C.'s
National Tourism Administration.
1998. Her hanging

may be revisionist history;

governments have trouble acknowledging P.T.S.D.

Why not give up on life?

Why continue to live?

I make up reasons why live on:

1. Kill myself, and I set a bad example

to children and everyone who knows me.

2. I will die deliberately, as Thoreau lived

deliberately. I live nonviolently. So I shall not

kill myself by hanging or sword. If up

to me, I'll die by helium, and be awake during

the transition, like a Tibetan, who dies with eyes open.

3. I have one more task to do—

translate and publish Father's poems.

In the tradition of poet answering poet,

BaBa wrote in the margins of my books.

With help from a scholar and the dictionary,

I'm able to read and hereby translate

his 19th song for barbarian reed pipe:

I can hear Mong Guo playing their music.

My horse sings a sad song in concert.

Some of those strange people are singing words;

some are playing instruments that double as

weapons, flutes to arrows, lyres to crossbows.

I can hear their voices outside
great walls. They are aliens to me,
though I am among / one of them. Alone.

But BaBa did not write "I."
The old poets did not write "I."

Hear Mong Guo playing their music.
Horse sings a sad song . . .
Hear their voices outside great walls . . .
They are aliens . . .
Among them, one alone.

But how be alone unless "I"? How
be lonely with you-understood alongside?
How be American unless "I"? Crossing
languages, crossing the sky of life and death,
Daughter will help Father. *I* am barbarian
who sings strange words. BaBa,
we'll show them, the academics who
can find no literature of South China.
We'll write dialect older and more tones
than Mandarin and Beijing. BaBa's
name-in-poetry is Lazy Old Man.
He was lucky, he got old.

He was wealthy with time,

to do nothing, to be poet.

4. Toward the end of her life, living alone,

MaMa accidently locked

herself out of the house, and spent the winter

night outside. She wrapped the old

dog blanket around herself, but could not

sleep. She walked around and around the house;

she tried lying down in various places

on the ground. She got up, and walked to the front

yard—and saw Kuan Yin on the porch.

The house looked like a resplendent altar; the porch

railings were altar rails. Kuan Yin was

watering the flowers and plants that adorned like spring,

red red green green. She stood

at the top of the stairs, and saw my mother. MaMa

knelt on the cement, and was warm with joy and beauty

and delight. Many many children came.

Kuan Yin and MaMa walked

among them, touching them on their bald heads.

When we found her, she was asleep

on the porch in a spot of morning sun.

5. I have the ability to sense love—it comes

from ancestors and family and sanghas of friends.

I am able to feel love from afar and ages ago.

6. Learn the patience to listen to music. Music
arranges time. Can't hurry listening.
I resolve to dance the Memorial Day
Carnaval in the Mission when I am 70.
7. I will have free time. I have never
had free time. I will have time to give away.
I regret always writing, writing. I gave
my kid the whole plastic bag of marshmallows,
so I could have 20 minutes to write.
I sat at my mother's deathbed, writing.
I did swab her mouth with water, and feel
her pliant tongue enjoy water, then harden
and die. Before I had language,

before I had stories, I wanted to write.
That desire is going away.
I've said what I have to say.
I'll stop, and look at things I called
distractions. Become reader of the world,
no more writer of it. Surely, world
lives without me having to mind it.
A surprise world! When I complete
this sentence, I shall begin taking
my sweet time to love the moment-to-moment
beauty of everything. Every one. Enow.

Glossary

ah—an honorific or vocative syllable, used in front of names, like "san" following names in Japanese

ahn—peace

'aina—land, earth

aiya—an interjection vocalized to express amazement, pain, sorrow, any emotion large or small

aloha kākou—"May there be love including all of us."

'ama'ama—mullet fish

aswang—an evil vampirelike creature living in the Philippines

'aumākua—totem animal; a familiar; an ancestor deified in the form of an animal

auwe—an interjection vocalized to express amazement, pain, sorrow, any emotion large or small

aw—a sound made at the end of a sentence indicating a question

Ba T'ien Ma Day—"Father Sky Mother Earth"; *Ba Tiān Ma Di* in Mandarin

big family—everybody, *tout le monde*

bow—bun, sweet or savory

casita—little house

chi—life's energy, *prana* in India, *ahshay* in West Africa

daw jeah; daw jay; dough zheh—"many thanks," in various dialects

deem—to judge, to ransom (in English); to mark, to consider (in Chinese)

dui—agree, match, aligned, paired

enow—enough

> A Book of Verses underneath the Bough,
> A Jug of Wine, a Loaf of Bread,—and Thou
> Beside me singing in the Wilderness—
> Oh, Wilderness were Paradise enow!
>
> —OMAR KHAYYAM

enso—circle, symbolizing the moment, the all, enlightenment, emptiness

este grupo, ese grupo—this group, that group

fawn—play

fawn (different ideogram from above)—cooked rice

feng shui—wind water

fu—human, bitter, tiger, pants, wolf's bane, or father, depending on tone

fu ngoy—fermented tofu

gaw—elder brother

goak goong—bow, obeisance (literally: nourish, cherish grandfather)

goong—grandfather

hai—yes

haole—white person; formerly, any foreigner

hapa—person of mixed blood; fraction

ho—good, very; *hao* in Mandarin

ho chau—very mean, most unkind

ho chun—very related

ho kin—good seeing you; well met

hola; ho, la—hello; good

ho'ohaole—to act like a white person

ho sun—good morning, good body, strongly believe, or good letter, depending on tones and context

huang dai—king (literally: yellow emperor)

hui—club, organization, association, society, band, team, troupe, league, firm, union, company, alliance

hun—regret, yearn, longing, hungry for

inmigrante—immigrant

jawk—capture

jeah jeah; je je; jeh jeh—"thanks thanks," in various dialects

je je nay; je je nee—"thank you," in various dialects

jing ho—to make good, to fix

joong—tamale, but wrapped with ti or banana or bamboo leaves rather than corn husks

joy kin; joy keen—*au revoir, auf Wiedersehen;* "zaijian," in village dialects

kuleana—responsibility, right, business, property, province, privilege, authority

kuleana hana—responsibilities on the job

kung—work, achievement; the time it takes in doing a piece of work

la; lah; law—a pleasant sound made at the end of a sentence

La Dona Guerrera—the Woman Warrior

la inmigración—immigration

lai—come

lan—orchid

las madres y las comadres—the mothers and godmothers

lei see—red packet of money (literally: come be), traditionally spelled *lai see*

lei see dai gut—gift of big luck, traditionally spelled *lai see dai gut*

li—tradition, rites, good manners:

> *Li* is the acting out of veneration and love, not only for parents, for one's sovereign, for one's people, but also for "Heaven-and-earth." . . . One learns by *Li* to take one's place gratefully in the cosmos and in history.
>
> —THOMAS MERTON

liang—pretty

lick—strength

loon—chaos

los derechos de criadas—the rights of maids

lu—road

mai—rice that is growing (Rice that is cooked is *fawn.*)

mai'a mālei—fish guardian from Makapu'u to Hanauma on O'ahu; "malei" for short

mele—song, anthem, chant, poem, poetry

mew; mow—"cat," in various dialects

mew (different ideogram from above)—temple

mien—face

minamina—regret a loss

ming—bright

mm—no, not

mo—a sound at the end of a sentence signifying a question

moy—younger sister, plum

ngum cha—drink tea

Nosotros no cruzamos la frontera; la frontera nos cruza.—"We do not cross the border; the border crosses us." (A slogan of the immigrants' rights movement)

paniolo—cowboy (after España, Spain)

Pásame la botella.—"Pass me the bottle."

pila ho'okani—instrumental music

po—grandmother

sammosa—forgetfulness; loss of awareness

sangha—the sacred community that lives in peace and harmony

Say Yup—language spoken in Four Districts, Guangzhou

seh doc—to bear; to afford; to be able to withstand

sing dawn fai lock— "Happy New Year" in Chinese (literally: holy birthday happiness joy)

sipapu—a small hole in the floor of the kiva symbolizing the portal through which the ancestors came

su doc—think virtue

suey yeah—midnight snack

sun—morning, body, believe, letter

tet nguyen dân—"Happy New Year" in Vietnamese (literally: feast of the first morning)

thala—ultimate star

ting—pavilion, sacred vessel, stop, listen

walk mountain—pay respects to the dead

waw; wei—interjections like "wow"

wu wei—non-doing

> Contentment and well-being at once become possible the moment you cease to act with them in view, and if you practice non-doing (*wu wei*), you will have both happiness and well-being.
>
> —THOMAS MERTON

Xizang—Tibet

zaijian—*au revoir, auf Wiedersehen*

Notes

Many thanks to the authors of the following sources, which are excerpted or referred to in the text:

Irving Berlin, "Sittin' in the Sun (Countin' My Money)."

Dalai Lama, *How to Expand Love: Widening the Circle of Loving Relationships,* translated by Jeffrey Hopkins, Atria Books, 2006.

Gilgamesh, translated by David Ferry, Farrar, Straus and Giroux, 1992.

Omar Khayyam, *Rubaiyat of Omar Khayyam,* translated by Edward Fitzgerald, 1858.

Thomas Merton, *The Way of Chuang Tzu,* New Directions, 1965.

John Mulligan, *Shopping Cart Soldiers,* Curbstone Press, 1997.

Rumi, "Songs of the Reed," *The Essential Rumi,* translated by Coleman Barks, Castle Books, 1997.

Maghiel van Crevel, *Chinese Poetry in Times of Mind, Mayhem, and Money,* Brill Academic Publishers, 2008.

Walt Whitman, *Leaves of Grass,* Sherman and Co., Philadelphia, 1900.

Yang Lian, "Poets and Poems in Exile: On Yang Lian, Wang Jiaxin, and Bei Dao," translated by Maghiel van Crevel.

CHINA MEN

Woven from memory, myth, and fact—a jour-
ney into the hearts and minds of Chinese men in
America: the grandfather who slaved in the Sierra
Nevadas on the transcontinental railroad . . . the
father who danced down Fifth Avenue, like Fred
Astaire, on days off from the laundry . . . and the
son who returned to China to find release from
his dead mother's angry spirit. Here is an accom-
plished storyteller's remarkably beautiful tale of
what they endured in a strange new land.

Nonfiction/Literature

THE FIFTH BOOK OF PEACE

A long time ago in China, there existed three Books
of Peace that proved so threatening to the reign-
ing powers that they had them burned. Many years
later, Maxine Hong Kingston wrote a Fourth Book
of Peace, but it too was burned—in the catastroph-
ic Berkeley–Oakland Hills fire of 1991, a fire that
coincided with the death of her father. Now in this
visionary and redemptive work, Kingston com-
pletes her interrupted labor, weaving fiction and
memoir into a luminous meditation on war and
peace, devastation and renewal.

Memoir/Literature

TRIPMASTER MONKEY

Wittman Ah Sing is a young Chinese-American hippie in San Francisco during the late sixties. Named after America's quintessential poet, indomitably garrulous and free-spirited, Wittman is as American as James Dean. Yet he also bears a striking resemblance to Monkey, the trickster-saint of Chinese legend who helped bring the Buddhist scriptures from India. Driven by his dream of writing and staging an epic production of interwoven Chinese novels and folk tales, Wittman's life becomes an extraordinary journey through an era as fantastic as his ambition—told in a novel by turns surreal, exuberantly charged with spectacle, violence, and Chinese "talk-story," and wildly, bitterly funny.

Fiction/Literature

ALSO AVAILABLE
The Woman Warrior